TELECULT POWER

THE AMAZING NEW WAY TO PSYCHIC AND OCCULT WONDERS

REESE P. DUBIN

PARKER
PUBLISHING COMPANY

parkerpub.co

www.parkerpub.co

To My Friends Who Made This Possible, Thank You

WHAT THIS BOOK WILL DO FOR YOU

What is Telecult Power? It is mental telepathy—plus. It is a power which you now possess, although you may not realize it. It is your power to bring about any desired goal you have—whether it be wealth, love, or power—easily, silently, by unobserved means!

Telecult Power means, literally, hidden distance power. It is based on the fact that there is a third form of energy, a human form of energy. Moreover, it is a form of intelligence that transcends death. With electrical energy and atomic energy, our books will soon be listing *Psychic Energy!*

HOW TELECULT POWER WORKS

What this means to you is this: every thought you think—whether in words or pictures—is reproduced exactly in the electron atmosphere around us. To put it another way, the psychic energy which is present in your brain spins off, or exudes, parts of itself into the electron atmosphere around us. What it spins off are sound waves and visual images in the embryonic state. Under ordinary conditions, these mental sights and sounds cannot be seen with the naked eye, or heard as sound is normally heard, but with Telecult Power they are revealed!

Not only do you generate and send out thought-forms, but you also act as a magnet that draws to you the thoughts of others.

All day long, whether you care to admit it or not, you are constantly being influenced by the thoughts of others. Most of this influence is unintentional. Some is deliberate. You will learn how to deal with both in these pages.

A MENTAL EARPHONE THAT LETS YOU HEAR THE THOUGHTS OF OTHERS!

Ever wonder when you look at someone: "What's he thinking?" If only you could *hear* what thoughts are going on in other people's minds, how fascinating and revealing it would be.

Impossible? Don't be too sure. In the next few pages, I intend to prove to your satisfaction that mind reading really does exist. I will even show you how to make and use an actual earphone—a Mental Earphone—that lets you hear the thoughts of others.

> **Once you actually begin receiving the thoughts of others, unknown to them, you will be very excited. With this Mental Earphone—which you can carry around with you—you will find that you can actually "hear" the unspoken thoughts of any person who happens to be standing near you.**

Your Mental Earphone can help you get along with others. It can help you understand a wife, a husband, or a son or daughter better. It can even help you find the perfect mate. It can make your life richer, fuller, happier.

A PSYCHIC TELE-VIEWER THAT LETS YOU SEE BEYOND WALLS!

In these pages, you'll discover how to make and use a wonderful psychic instrument—called a Tele-Viewer—that can help you see beyond walls and over great distances! With this and the Mental Earphone, I'll show you . . .

- **How you may see and hear through solid walls, and over great distances! Pick up actual sights and sounds, through Telecult Power!**
- **How you can discover hidden treasures and large sums of money—gold, silver, diamonds and jewels —money in cash, stocks or bonds hidden under a floor board or in the ground. Even treasure sealed behind ordinary walls!**
- **How you may use it as a "Tele-Photo Transmitter" to teleport the object of your desire to you, from the invisible world!**

Yes, you'll see how to bring your desire—called a Photo-Form—into focus and "photograph" it psychically. Once this happens, it slowly materializes for you to see, feel, touch and possess! *You'll see how a woman used this method to materialize a man-servant out of thin air!*

But that's the least of it! Think for a moment of what this means to you! It means that you can never be cheated, tricked, or misled!

You'll see how your Psychic Tele-Viewer may be used to take advantage of money opportunities long before they are made public! Many a low-paid worker has risen to wealth simply by "tuning in" on the minds of his bosses and superiors. Shopkeepers have also been able to use it to double, triple and quadruple their incomes—simply because they always know how to please their customers, through information received with this instrument. Fortunes have been made with it!

HOW TO BROADCAST TELE-COMMANDS THAT MUST BE OBEYED WITH THE AMAZING HYPNO-PHONE!

Here is a method that actually enables you to influence the thoughts of others, by silent, unobserved means.

No one can escape the power of this method. The law is absolute. Everybody, high or low, rich or poor, ignorant or wise, all are subject to its spell!

This method may be used to impel a customer to buy; to double your friends and double your money; to command someone to sleep; to make someone get up and come to you; to bring your mate to you without asking; to make a friend or relative contact you; to influence a total stranger and interest him in your well-being; to convert a dreaded enemy into a loyal friend; and much more!

It can work in as little as 10 seconds flat!

HOW TO JOIN THE HIDDEN BROTHERHOOD AND ENJOY A WONDERFUL NEW LIFE OF MONEY, FRIENDS, AND POWER

You'll see how you may join a secret organization known as the Hidden Brotherhood. You'll see how members of this organization can get anything they want, for any member of the group. It's like an **Insta-Matic Dial-a-Wish Service** that actually works!

You'll discover . . .

- **The Secret Ceremonies of the Hidden Brotherhood!**
- **The Complete List of Secret Group Chants!**
- **The Magic Money Chant!**
- **The Magic Chant to Make You Look and Stay Young!**
- **The Magic Chant for Finding a Perfect Mate!**

- **The Magic Chant to Make a Child or Spouse Obedient!**
- **How every member of your group can get anything he wants!**

Do not wait for tomorrow, next week, or next month to join the Hidden Brotherhood. There isn't any reason in the world why you shouldn't enjoy the riches, the happiness, the radiant health and peace of mind God meant for you to enjoy *now!*

You need no special abilities, education, or psychic "gifts" to join the Hidden Brotherhood. Men and women, old and young —all are welcome You'll find the full details in these pages

HOW TO MAKE AND USE "A MAGIC MONEY BAG" TO RECEIVE GIFTS FROM THE INVISIBLE WORLD!

You'll see why scientists are now convinced that there exists an invisible world—a world where objects and very lifelike beings exist—which seems to be the framework around which our own world is built!

You'll see how to make and use a remarkable device with which to receive gifts from this world—gifts such as gold, silver, diamonds, platinum, and much more. I'll show you how to use . . .

- **A "Psychic Lantern" that lights up the invisible world to let you see people and events in a future of your choice!**
- **A "Spirit Compass" to help you recognize Cosmic Signs!**
- **The Signs of Love!**
- **The Signs of Money!**
- **A Complete List of Omens!**
- **500 Dreams Revealed!**
- **25 Lucky Numbers for You!**

And still that's just the beginning! I want to tell you all about it, because right now, everything you need is in this invisible world—money, jewels, servants, fine possessions—everything, waiting for you to call upon them, to materialize into solid reality for you *to see, touch, and possess!*

A LIFETIME PLAN FOR TELECULT POWER!

This book presents what amounts to a lifetime plan for Telecult Power: a push-button technique that can be applied automatically to get you what you want in any situation. It's like a Psychic Generator or Duplicating Machine that turns your dreams into solid reality.

Set the dial on riches and a host of magic money-making techniques are here, all ready to work for you. Push your mental "On" button by opening the pages of this book and you'll discover:

- **A Magic Street where you can go where pennies actually fall from the sky, every day, in great quantities. People have picked up as many as 1,000 in less than an hour!**
- **A "Mental Levitating Finger" you can use to move objects without touching them, and how you can use it in games of chance, such as the calling of dice, the operation of a roulette wheel—and even in games of skill, such as billiards, bowling and golf!**
- **An actual Money Compass that will lead you to undreamed-of wealth and happiness!**

You are now on the verge of the most rewarding experience of your life. In a very short time, the startling secrets of Telecult Power will be placed in your hands! Just as a magician's wand was said to work miracles, so too will this book enable you to experience wonder after wonder!

Now, for the first time, you will be able to control that mysterious force which some call magic, some call mind power, and still others call the divinity in man.

—The Author

CONTENTS

TELECULT POWER #1

YOUR MENTAL EARPHONE:

How to Hear the Thoughts of Others

Ever wonder when you look at someone: "What's he thinking?" If only you could *hear* what thoughts are going on in other people's minds, how fascinating and revealing it would be.

You could never be tricked or misled. In a social situation, you would know instantly whether the other party really liked you, what kind of impression you were making, whether he or she were sincere. And in business, with Mind Reading, there would be no limit to the things you could do. During a job interview, for example, you could get a glowing recommendation—since you would know exactly what the personnel man was waiting for you to say. And your advancement would be meteoric!

Impossible? Don't be too sure. In the next few pages, I intend to prove to your satisfaction that Mind Reading really does exist, and that:

> **Thoughts, the thoughts you think, do not need to be spoken in order to be heard. Just as everyone in the world would hear the same sound if you spoke it,**

anyone who knows the secret can hear your words
as you think them.

This can be done in two ways. First, this sound can be sent out in the form of subvocalization (slight vibrations of the throat, altered by movements of the tongue), which can be picked up by a psychic or sensitive person.

Secondly, speech can be transferred directly from your mind to the mind of another person. This is accomplished as follows: Speech is formed in the auditory center of your brain which "hears" what you say before you say it. The mechanism is similar to dreaming, in which the eyeballs of the dreamer can be seen moving behind the eyelids in a visual hallucination. Something very similar happens in Telecult Hearing. The sound is "tested" against the eardrum before it is uttered.

In this process, the eardrum is used, not to receive sound from the outside, but to receive sound from the inside, sound in its embryo stage, which is "heard" by the thinker in an auditory hallucination. Tongue and throat muscles aid in this process.

That sound can be produced from your mind has been proven by physiologists, according to author Frank R. Young: "While testing a decerebrate animal (one in which all its brain, except for the cerebellum and the lower projections of the temporal lobe, has been removed) they found, to their utter disbelief, spoken words and other sounds were *faithfully reproduced* when electrodes were placed upon the auditory nerve and connected with a telephone receiver or loud speaker." *

Thus, it becomes more believable that the human mind can produce sounds as well as receive them. In fact the human ear, which transmits sounds to the brain, is remarkably like a microphone, which transmits sounds into a telephone, or into a radio,

* Frank R. Young, *Cyclomancy: The Secret of Psychic Power Control* (West Nyack, N.Y.: Parker Publishing Co., Inc., 1966).

or into a tape recorder. Theoretically, it should be able to produce sound as well as receive it. You can get a clearer understanding of this if you have a tape recorder handy.

If you plug the microphone into the "in-put" hole and talk, your words will be recorded on tape. If you play back the tape, your words will come out of the speaker on the machine. But if you suddenly plug the microphone into the "out-put" hole on the machine, the words will stop coming out of the loudspeaker and will come out of the microphone, exactly as if it were the earpiece on a telephone.

The mechanical equipment needed for reception of radio sound waves is really very simple. During the Second World War, many soldiers who were in prison camps reported that they were able to pick up Allied radio broadcasts with nothing more than an egg shell, a wire and a rusty razor blade. Thousands of early homemade sets consisted of little more. We also hear occasional news stories of people who receive radio programs through metal fillings in their teeth, or through apparently normal ears!

Your cerebral equipment is much like early radio sets. The entire surface of the brain is covered with tiny specks of nerve tissue that are sensitive to all electrical charges near them.

The sound issuing from the sender does not have to be audible. It can be many decibels above human hearing, like radio waves before they reach your radio set. All that is necessary is for this "sound" to hit the outer atmosphere, to create a wave or vibration in the electron sea around us. This *can* be picked up by another mind, through sensitive neurons (nerve cells) in the skin, eyes and ears.

YOUR MENTAL EARPHONE

In a sense, the Telecult Power which you and I and everyone possess to "hear" what other people are thinking may be described as or compared with an earphone—a Mental Earphone which you carry around with you. Once you have learned how to use this Earphone, you may use it to great personal advantage.

I will even show you how to make and use an actual earphone, one that you hold to your ear, that aids in this process. I even like to think of the pages of this book as channels of communication, like the bands on a radio dial, and I want you to do the same.

Thus, if I say, tune in to Telecult Power #1 and discover how the Mental Earphone can reveal a woman's secret thoughts, simply turn to page 36 of this chapter and "tune in" on the evidence.

In a subsequent chapter (Telecult Power #4), you will see how the Mental Earphone may be used by two people for Telephone Telepathy, as in the following example.

A TWO-WAY CONVERSATION FROM NEW YORK TO CALIFORNIA WITH THE AMAZING MENTAL EARPHONE

An acquaintance of mine, Samuel N., reports how he made use of this Mental Earphone in a scientifically controlled experiment, with a friend in California. At an appointed time, the experiment began.

Speaking aloud, and addressing his friend in California, he said: "Please take any book or magazine handy, tell me the name of it, and read a few words from it, at random, citing the exact page."

My friend states that a few moments later he was able to clearly hear the following reply: "I will read you a passage from page 5 of a book called *Modern Spiritualism.*" He then read the passage.

By long-distance telephone, from New York to California, it was immediately found that all had happened exactly as my friend describes it. The man in California heard my friend's request, word for word. And my friend dictated the reply—

as he received it—onto a dictaphone, together with the exact hour and date, to preserve the evidence.

A STAGE COURSE IN MIND READING

During the course of the next few pages, you will learn many of the most treasured mind reading secrets of professional stage performers. Men who have accurately told perfect strangers personal facts about themselves, naming names, places, facts, figures and dates—who have accurately described the contents of sealed envelopes and locked steel safes, known only to others. These genuine mind reading demonstrations can be duplicated by anyone who knows how. And since *Telecult Power* shows you how, this book is, in a sense, a kind of stage course in mind reading.

Once you actually begin receiving the thoughts of others—unknown to them—you will be very excited, and you will never be satisfied to leave this book until you have become a perfect master at it.

However, with this power comes great responsibility. You must never use your knowledge to hurt other people. For there is an unwritten Law of the Universe which says that whatever harm you cause others will be done unto you.

HOW I DISCOVERED THE MENTAL EARPHONE

To repeat, then, this is a power that you already possess, just like sight, hearing, taste, touch and smell. Unlike the others, however, it needs to be trained. Otherwise, it will only "help out" now and then, when you unconsciously do something to make it work. As a matter of fact, that's how I found out about the Mental Earphone. From time to time I would have little telepathic experiences—just as we all do—and as a sort of hobby, I tried to recall just what I was doing when the experience occurred.

Soon, I was actually able to hear what other people were thinking. At first these hearing impressions startled me, and I would take them for actual speech, until I realized that people don't usually say such things out loud.

In the beginning, of course, my experiences were far less dramatic. They were, in fact, quite ordinary. Here are some of them. See if you can guess the secret, which I will reveal immediately afterward.

MENTAL EARPHONE SAYS: "DO NOT BUY HOUSE!"

I was a boy of perhaps fifteen. My parents were in the market for a new house. After many long months of "looking," we had finally settled on a "bargain." As the owners were discussing terms with my parents, a feeling of uneasiness crept over me. Something suddenly told me that the owner and his wife were pulling a fast one on us. As it later turned out, there was a boundary dispute which the owners were trying to conceal.

MENTAL EARPHONE BRINGS GOOD JOB

Later, when I was in college and needed a job, the college placement office sent me to one of the most unusual job interviews I ever had. I seemed to know everything the man wanted to hear, and I said it—and got the job over five other applicants sitting in the waiting room.

MESSAGE TRAVELS 3,000 MILES!

Not long afterward, another event occurred which I can only attribute to telepathy. While having supper one evening, I remembered an event which happened when I was about six years old. And a name and face were immediately brought to mind. The following day, lo and behold, a letter came from this very individual.

HOW TO USE THE MENTAL EARPHONE

As I say, I made notes. After each thought-receiving experience I wrote down exactly what I had been doing at the time. After a while, when I compared these notes, I discovered one item that appeared every time. Here it is . . .

Relaxation. In the case of the house, I was relaxed and in good spirits when the feeling came over me. The job that I was applying for was one well suited to my abilities, and I was at ease during the interview. In the third example, I was enjoying supper when the "message" came.

In every instance, I was completely at ease. This, I have discovered, is the most important secret in receiving other people's thoughts. But I soon discovered that there was something about relaxation that I didn't know, because the next time I consciously tried to relax to receive another person's thoughts, nothing happened. What had gone wrong? After much experimentation, I discovered the phenomenon of Deep Relaxation.

Most people think that they can relax completely—as I thought—when actually they cannot. If you want to see if you can relax completely, try this experiment.

Retire to a quiet room, and try to blank out all conscious thought, looking steadily at some simple object directly in your line of vision.

Now close your eyes and try to visualize the object in your mind. If you can still see the object several seconds after your eyes are closed, it means you have relaxed completely. If the object fades from your mind, it means you are not relaxed, that your mind is being distracted by other sights, sounds or thoughts.

Most people's minds are like this, flitting from image to image, thought to thought. With the mind racing this way, it is not possible to receive other people's thoughts.

In Deep Relaxation, it's not that your thinking is different—

it's that it practically ceases. Being completely relaxed and detached, you become like a hollow tube through which the message flows.

Before I give you the technique of Deep Relaxation, let us consider for a moment what relaxation is *not*. In the first place, it is *not* play. Nor is it a change of pace or of occupation. A "change of pace" is merely substituting one form of activity for another. The mind keeps ticking away, the muscles remain at work.

Deep relaxation—relaxation as it should be—is the ability to blank out all thoughts, and to relax every muscle in your body. To be quite frank, if you want to be able to receive other people's thoughts at will, you need to be able to relax at will, so completely that you aren't even aware of the clothes on your body. Easy-does-it is the watchword here, for you are much more likely to achieve your goal if you don't try too hard.

STEP ONE

Until you have become so adept at Deep Relaxation that you can start it any time at will, your period of relaxation should be taken away from other people, in a room where you are alone, with the door closed. Choose a quiet place, so as not to be distracted. If you live in the city, you cannot avoid a certain amount of noise, but try to control what sounds you can, since conversation, the radio, the ticking of a clock can be most distracting.

Your clothes should be comfortable, too. In fact, the less you have on the better. Any tight-fitting garments should be loosened. But be sure there are no drafts in the room. It is impossible to relax while chilly.

The best position for Deep Relaxation is flat on your back on the floor, using a rug or folded blanket as a mattress. Otherwise, you should use a hard bed, preferably with a bed board.

A soft bed is bad because, as it sags, many of your muscles will tense up.

At first, you may not feel entirely comfortable like this. The floor or bed board will feel too hard, and you will find yourself tempted to shift positions. But this you must not do, for in order to relax muscle by muscle it is important to lie quite still. Just remember that any body movement, however slight, means a tensing of one or another group of muscles.

Once settled, take a few deep breaths. Draw your chest straight upward. Exhale slowly and relax. Repeat three or four times. Then allow yourself to breathe normally again.

STEP TWO

The next step is to get acquainted with the *feel* of your muscles so that you may better control them. To do this, start by stretching an arm or a leg. Stretch hard, making all the muscles along the way contract—and study what is happening. You will feel other muscles, far away, tensing up in sympathy. If you clench your fist, for example, you will feel muscles tensing all the way up your arm and into your shoulder. If you clench your toes, your thigh muscles will tense up, too. Repeat this process limb by limb, until you can instantly recognize tension anywhere in your body. You will need to be able to banish it at will.

STEP THREE

Now start the stretching all over again, but this time in slow motion, like a cat arching its back. Observe and note your sensations. Hold the pose until you are thoroughly aware of what is happening. Then, slowly, let go.

It is this letting-go process that is the actual mechanism of true relaxation.

For your daily practice, it has been found that the most effective way to relax is to begin at the top and work down. Relax the head first—let go the face muscles, the jaw muscles, the eyeballs, the lips, the tongue, the neck and so on—by tensing up and letting go. Fifteen minutes to a half-hour a day will do, at first. Later on reduce to ten-minute periods, or whenever your body feels ready to get back into action. Remember, however, never to get up hastily, or you will be undoing the benefits of this technique.

After a while relaxation will become a habit and you will no longer need to think of specific areas of the body. You will be able to relax at will, completely unnoticed, any time, any place.

HOW TO "TUNE IN" WITH HYPERACUITY

Having learned how to keep the body subdued and the mind as free of thoughts as possible, it is necessary to sensitize the mind and body, to practice *recognizing* mental and physical impressions other than your own. For example . . .

One of the ways to develop the heightened sensitivity—called "hyperacuity"—needed for mind reading is through Contact Telepathy. Many years ago, when the Society for Psychical Research in London first began investigating mind reading, they discovered this method.

Contact Telepathy, as the name would imply, involves touching the person whose mind you want to read. If you use this method discreetly—after much practice—it is possible to pick up thoughts with unbelievable clarity.

THE SKIN AS AN ELECTRICAL CONDUCTOR OF SOUND

The reason is simple. Sound waves that are emitted from the body (visual impressions, too) are nowhere near strong enough to be heard without special preparation. Subvocalized words, perhaps, but not thought-sounds (which are equivalent to radio signals before they reach your radio). A radio has condensers and other equipment to strengthen the weak radio waves it receives in the air and make them discernible.

By sensitizing the skin with Contact Telepathy, you get a similar effect. The surface area of your body (which also has millions of nerve ends or antennae) becomes extremely sensitive to the surrounding atmosphere, and to electrical impulses within this atmosphere.

RECEIVING THOUGHTS THROUGH TOUCH

It begins with muscle reading, and is the process whereby tiny muscle movements—and eventually actual thoughts—are detected by touching another person.

Contact Telepathy is basically quite easy. One system is for the demonstrator to grip the subject's wrist, right upon left, or vice versa. Another is for the demonstrator and the subject to lock arms, rather loosely, either left to right or vice versa. Still another way is for the mind reader to have contact with *two* subjects, each concentrating on the same thought, whose minds he will read. After some practice, it will no longer be necessary for you to follow these instructions exactly. Nor will it be necessary for you to have a willing subject on whom to practice.

You should eventually reach the point where the instant you touch someone on the shoulder, for example, you will receive his thoughts. Contact Telepathy is a fascinating pastime. One simple way for you to appreciate it is to try it yourself. Proceed as follows:

NUMBER ONE: FINDING HIDDEN OBJECTS

Ask a good friend to blindfold you with a handkerchief, or turn away from him. Then request him to hide something, such as a knife, a paper weight or a pencil, in a well-concealed place within the room.

Now, after he has concealed the thing, tell him: "One thing that is necessary for a successful demonstration is that you must first lend me your hand. The second is that you must keep your whole attention fixed upon the place where the knife is hidden, then upon the knife itself. I should be able to discover where it is hidden."

Then take hold of his right hand with your left hand and completely relax. Loosen all the muscles of your hand and be ready to observe even the least motion or vibration of his hand. In case you do not notice any such movements of his hand, suggest to him firmly: "Think! Keep your mind only on where the knife lies." Immediately, move a step forward. You do this to make the guide impart a vibratory motion unconsciously to your hand, which is a sure and sufficient clue to allow yourself to move along that direction. If you get no vibration, step back and move in an opposite direction, one step. The vibrations or muscular movements you will start to receive should be of two types. Either a pull back, which clearly indicates to you that the direction in which you were moving is wrong, or a noticeable "leading on" of your hand—completely unconscious on the part of the other person. In either case, the muscular movement of your friend's hand is your key and leading instrument to the place where the knife is. Bear in mind that the more intense the concentration of *his* mind is on the knife, the more you are sure to succeed in finding it.

• • •

Now you will try to find a concealed pin. To make the experiment easier, it is better to have two guides instead of one. Request them to encircle your neck with their four hands so that the thumbs of the hands of each guide touch each other, and the little fingers of each hand touch each other. This way you have the benefit of two concentrating minds, so you can receive plenty of impulses and nerve indications for a move.

Step by step, move as you are guided by the unconscious action of the guides. To help you relax, it is best to keep your eyes closed as much as possible. As you near the place where the object is hidden, you will receive a distinct impulse directing you to stop. It may then be possible for you to notice, by feeling a gentle downward pressure on your shoulders, whether you should stoop down to pick up the object. Your friends will be baffled and amazed. They will also be greatly impressed and will unconsciously aid you in further experiments.

> **The real purpose of these experiments, however, is not to entertain—although it is entertaining—but rather to train your mind to pick up the tiniest sensations possible. In the tests just given, it was muscle movement—ever so slight. But it is a short jump from the perception of tiny muscle movement to receiving actual thoughts.**

The tests for finding a concealed object (Number One) must be tried a number of times with various articles until you become a master at it, before proceeding to the following exercises.

NUMBER TWO: PICK THE BOOK

This is an advanced version of "finding a concealed object." In this case, no blindfold is needed, and the object is known in advance. It is a book, but the question is, which book? The test is worked in a room with a large or fair-sized bookcase. One volume is taken out and replaced during your absence by a friend (or while several friends look on).

When you come back into the room, ask your friend or friends to concentrate firmly on the book that has been chosen. Then take the hand of the one who picked the book in your absence.

Standing near the bookcase with this person, gently swing his hand back and forth, while running your free hand back and forth along a row of books. If you receive no impulse from your friend's hand, try the row of books above or below, until you are certain that you feel an impulse or vibration from his hand. (If you have touched the wrong shelf, you may even feel a slight upward or downward movement of your friend's hand —completely unconscious on his part, telling you which shelf to go to.)

When you receive a definite twitch or squeezing sensation from this person's hand, you will know that you are very close to touching the right book. Stop your hand as soon as you feel this "vibration." Now move your hand back and forth slightly along the books, right in the area where you receive a "muscle" impulse from your friend's hand (it is no longer necessary to move his hand back and forth; just hold it). Proceed very cautiously to do this, waiting for a slight impulse from his hand. When you receive this signal, stop. Your hand should be on the exact book he picked.

Another version of this experiment, slightly more difficult, is to ask your friend or friends to pick an actual page from the book—the first page of a chapter. Then, holding one person's hand, run your free hand down the list of chapters in the book's Table of Contents, pausing on each, until you get an impulse.

NOTE: Later, when you begin receiving actual thoughts, you will be able to have a friend select any word on any page in the entire book, and you will know it.

NUMBER THREE: HOW TO "READ" A WORD ON SOMEONE'S MIND

Provide yourself with a blackboard or any blank writing surface. Take hold of your friends's right hand with your left, and tell him to think of a word or name. He must concentrate hard on this word or name.

Now, with the chalk, crayon or pencil in your right hand, mark down lines according to the movement of your friend's hand. These scribblings, after a while, should start to take on recognizable form. If you carefully feel for the slight movement of your friend's hand—and draw the shape of what you feel with your hand, you are sure to reproduce your friend's mental image or thought. Your friend, whose thought you are reading, will assist you without knowing he is doing so.

NUMBER FOUR: RECEIVING A COMPLETE THOUGHT

You should definitely wait before trying this, until you have become an absolute master at detecting slight muscle movement. When you had success with each of the steps just given—proceed to this one, test Number Four.

> **This is the key step, the one where you begin to bridge the gap between receiving tiny muscle movement to receiving an actual thought. It is an extension of the first test—picking the object. It does not stop at that point, however. Instead, you must *do* something with the object—whatever the person whose mind you are reading decides for you to do.**

For example, he might "will" you to pick up a box of candy, open it, and offer some to specific persons present.

You proceed as before, by making actual contact with the person whose mind you are reading. However, this time, *both of you* must be absolutely calm and relaxed. If you have any doubts about your friend, instruct him in how to relax, or find someone who has a naturally relaxed personality. (A tense, nervous or jittery mind does not radiate thought well, except for fractions of a second. If your friend is tense, you, as a beginner, may miss the message.)

Now close your eyes and request your friend to hold your hand and think of what he wants you to do. Make your mind a blank and relax completely. Your friend, meanwhile, should be thinking of the first action he wants you to perform (for example: "Pick up the box of candy"). When you have received the thought, open your eyes and carry out the instruction. Then close your eyes and proceed as before, step by step, until you have completed each step.

As in earlier steps, you will sense a feeling of restraint in his hand if you start to do the wrong action; and you will get the "go-ahead" if you are right. *However, you should also start to get actual thought impressions (the words themselves that he is thinking, or a mental image of yourself doing such and such an action) quite independent of what you feel from your friend's hand.*

This experiment should be tried many times, on many different occasions. Always remember: both you and your friend must relax completely. When the feeling or thought impression comes over you, endeavor to *prolong* it, not by concentrating on it, but by becoming more relaxed. You will be rewarded for your patience by the welcome flow of thoughts—actual thoughts—from your friend's mind.

Try to master this before going on to the next section, "Receiving Thoughts Through Space." Meanwhile, here is another interesting experiment you can try.

NUMBER FIVE: THE BLINDFOLD DRIVE

This was a favorite of Washington Irving Bishop, the famous mind reader of the 1880's. He would drive through the streets blindfolded, with a horse and carriage, to some destination known only to a subject—or transmitter—who was riding with him. In recent years, people have done the same with automobiles.

However, you can try this test for yourself in a perfectly safe manner. Suppose that you are taking a person somewhere in your car, and he knows the way but you don't. Instead of having him tell you where to turn, how many blocks to go, and so on, have him rest his hand on your shoulder or arm and keep thinking ahead, step by step. Often you can pick up the impressions so perfectly that you can pull up in front of the exact house he has in mind.

This can be worked the other way around. With someone else driving the car and thinking of the route, you can sit beside him, resting your hand on his arm, and call the turns before he comes to them.

THE FIRST HINT THAT YOU HAVE BEEN SUCCESSFUL

Incredible as it may seem, soon you will be able to actually feel the pressure of a sound wave against your opened hands. To quote Frank R. Young: "When a sound wave of a frequency beyond that which you can hear easily, reaches (you), it will be felt by the skin of your hands and conveyed to your Sensations Recording Center. From there it will be automatically relayed to your cortex (your conscious and subconscious minds), and your cortex will instinctively command the muscles of your hands to react to the pressure against them by withdrawing suddenly, such as by jerking ever so slightly. . . ." *

To test this, he recommends that you lie awake at night and listen for the faintest sounds you can. He recommends that you relax and lie as quietly as possible. If you have been successful in developing your hyperacuity through Contact Telepathy and other methods recommended here, *then you will be able to "hear" sound with your muscles before there is a perceptible sound in your ear.*

"You will not hear the sound with your hand," he says, "but you will feel 'something coming on.' Your muscles will flex the slightest and thereby warn you of the sound even before your ears respond to the slightest inkling of it. You have given your

* Frank R. Young, *Cyclomancy: The Secret of Psychic Power Control.*

muscles 'ears.' The blind man develops this ability to an abnormal degree."

MENTAL EARPHONE REVEALS WOMAN'S SECRET THOUGHTS

In the preceding experiment, in the case of human thought, even if the impulse proves too faint to be heard by ear, and too weak to be heard with the Mental Earphone, it is still registered in that portion of your cortex known as the subconscious mind. This can be proven by what I call the Tele-Pen method —placing a pencil in your hand at the precise moment when you feel that "something coming on." It will record what you have unconsciously heard.

If you wish to read someone's mind, for example, you have merely to "tune in" by thinking of this person. Some years ago, an English journalist had an unusual experience of this nature.

One day, after a hectic day at work, he sat down to relax and began to think about a woman friend with whom he wished to dine. Wondering what her plans might be (these were the days before telephones were in common use) he decided to write her a note. Taking a pen and placing it on a sheet of paper, suddenly—to his utter disbelief—his hand began writing of its own accord! This was the message:

> I love you, my dear, from the first time I set eyes on you. Even though I've never said so, in as many words, and may have led you to believe, at times, that I was standoffish, you are always on my mind. You have a certain way about you . . . I think of you constantly. . . . Why don't you call me? Why can't you *hear* me? I'm at my sister's house in Brighton. . . . *Brighton*. Please try to remember.

He was flabbergasted at what he had just written. What could have come over him? Was it fanciful thinking or a true psychic experience of some sort? He wrote his friend a hasty note, asking if she had been thinking of him as he had of her that particular evening, and would she care to dine with him.

Her reply, arriving in record time, expressed amazement at the coincidence, and said that yes, she had been thinking of him and recalling how pleasant their previous date had been . . . although she gave no hint of her true thoughts. She accepted the invitation, stating that she might be free the following Saturday.

RECEIVING THOUGHTS THROUGH SPACE

As was mentioned earlier, sounds can be uttered in the form of subvocalization; that is, murmured under the breath, often without opening the mouth, but simply by moving the teeth and the tongue inside and pretending, with air that passes up and out through the nose, to be speaking. As a matter of fact, many physiologists insist that this is the way most people think most of the time, even when they don't realize it.

Strange as it may seem, the murmured speech behind closed lips can be understood. But before this can happen, the actual hearing faculty must be sharpened. One method is to proceed as follows:

Exercise 1. Strain your ears to detect the individual sounds creeping through the chaos of jabber from a group of people. At first, you will catch only a syllable or two, or a word now and then. Distinctness will precede magnification. Slowly the individual sounds from the group will grow steadily more intense to you, as well as more distinct.

Exercise 2. Turn your radio or television set very low and listen to every word coming from it. Half a minute later turn it still lower and listen to it again. Continue until you can hardly hear it and concentrate on the faint words.

Exercise 3. When you are in bed, try to hear the faint breathing of someone asleep in another room, the rumble of a vehicle several blocks away, a distant bird, insect or animal.

Exercise 4. Listen to a clock or a wrist watch. Then move farther and farther away until you can hardly hear it. Now force yourself to hear it just as loudly as you did before.

Exercise 5. Plug your ears with hard-packed pellets of cotton a little bigger than the opening of your ear, and repeat each of the preceding exercises.

Remember, receiving thoughts is something that anyone can do, who is willing to try. However, it is only practice that makes perfect. You must not hurry over the practice in an effort to become a master of both time and space within a day. Easy tests should be tried at first, then gradually more difficult ones. The secret of success is always enthusiasm and earnest expectation. If you fail in the beginning, do not be discouraged, but keep at it until you get good results.

POWERFUL SECRETS OF MIND READING REVEALED!

Now, from the perception of subvocalized sound, you may proceed to the actual reception of thought from another mind, with no physical contact. Thought will pass directly from this person's mind into your own.

To begin with, observe these rules:

1. Remember that a calm, not-too-anxious mind functions best. Use Deep Relaxation for this purpose. Do not clench your fists or grind your teeth. Relax, completely and deeply, make your mind a blank, ready to receive any impression.
2. Enlist the aid of a friend or friends who are likewise relaxed and patient. It would be advantageous if these are the friends with whom you practiced Contact Telepathy.

Now I shall give you some powerful secrets of Mind Reading. Use them and you will succeed beyond your wildest dreams.

First of all, as a general rule, when reading the mind of a good acquaintance, try to think of all the qualities which he or she possesses. If you are standing face to face with the person, look at this person intently, from time to time, without making him feel uncomfortable. Try to get the "feel" of this person's personality, how he walks, talks and moves, his likes and dislikes, his temperament, how he reacts to different situations, what he's likely to be thinking about at this moment. Finally, when you are completely "attuned" to this person, relax, and you will find to your amazement *that the thoughts come.* To test the accuracy of the thoughts you receive, simply repeat them and your friend will exclaim: "That's right! That's exactly what I was thinking! Why, you must be telepathic!" Even a beginner can get such results.

Secondly, when attempting to read anyone's mind, always wait for those times when he or she seems most relaxed and "at ease with the world." If the person is smiling or humming to himself, *that* is a good time to start mind reading. If you happen to be speaking to this person and he seems contented or in a good mood, that, too, is a good time to read his thoughts. Similarly, you will find that the thoughts of others come to you with greatest clarity at those times when both you and the other person are in a good mood.

If possible, try to avoid reading the mind of someone who is troubled or upset, until your Telecult power has strengthened considerably from great use.

READING YOUR FRIEND'S MIND AT A DISTANCE

There are also some tricks you can use when practicing long-distance telepathy with a friend. If you are a beginner (assuming you want things as easy as possible), plan to practice in the early morning, late afternoon, or at night.

The atmosphere around you is clearest at these times, free of radio waves that might interfere, as well as sunspot ions. You should especially practice receiving at dawn or earlier, since everyone's mind, including your own, is most relaxed at that time.

To practice, have your friend send you a brief message at this time (he may even be in another city). The message should be brief, but ask your friend to concentrate on it for at least a half-hour, without letup, willing that you will understand what it is. A good idea would be for your friend to have the message written out (printed) and to concentrate on it.

In order to tune in on this person, however, it will be necessary—in the beginning—to have a good idea of his or her physical surroundings. If possible, visit the place where he will be, and show this person your surroundings. Exchange photographs or pencil sketches of the rooms you will use. Memorize these pictures. Tell your friend to trace the two points between your homes with his finger on a map, and you do likewise. This process is somewhat like directing an antenna onto the right beam. Indeed, physiologists picture the brain as bearing near its outer surface billions of tiny nerve ends aimed as if they were aerials for directional radio.

A "HOMEMADE" ANTENNA THAT PICKS UP THOUGHTS

At the appointed hour, you should be holding—in your hand or elsewhere against bare skin—some bit of material which has been in close contact with the other party. (In the Polynesian Islands, those who wish to send or receive a telepathic message often try to obtain clippings of the person's hair or fingernails.)

> **Such a "homemade" antenna constitutes an actual link between minds across space, since all objects and creatures in existence emit radiations—tiny electrical currents that vibrate at the same rate as the object from which they arise. When you hold such an object, belonging to another person, against your body, you become more strongly attuned to his radiation—or "radio"—frequency.**

At the De La Warr Laboratories, Oxford, England, scientists have discovered, for example, that if a photograph is taken of an object, the photographic emulsion—or film—will be saturated with the same radiations as the object, and will continue to give off these radiations for some time afterwards. More startling still, these radiations seem to constitute an invisible channel between the object and the photograph, *linking* the two. For when the vibrations of various foods, such as water and minerals, are reproduced in an oscillator and beamed *at the photograph in the laboratory,* the plant is nourished without food! *

This secret, called "psychometry," may be used also in *sending* messages, since it helps constitute an actual telephone link between two people. But for now we are concerned with *receiving* other people's thoughts.

For your experiments, any small objects will do, such as a ring, a pin, an earring, or some trinket, a watch, a hairpin, keys, pen or pencil, a glove, tie or handkerchief—anything, as long as it has been in frequent or prolonged contact with the owner's body, or is an object at which he gazes frequently (such as some bauble or knickknack on a desk). Try to select objects belonging to your friend which have not been touched by anyone else.

While awaiting your friend's message, hold your hand against the object that belongs to him, or press your finger or palm against it. An object such as a watch, or a bracelet that fits snugly, may be fastened to your wrist. (It would be helpful, if you don't mind revealing this secret, if he were doing the same with an object belonging to you.) This will link your two personalities, by means of their radiation frequencies, across space. If, at any time, you should have trouble, ask yourself, "Am I trying too hard?" And if you are, try to forget the object of this experiment and relax.

Do not practice receiving while lying down or tired, lest you drowse. If you feel you may be tired at the appointed time,

* Reported in *The Ark* (Bulletin of the Catholic Study Circle for Animal Welfare), London, England, August 1955.

allow yourself a few minutes beforehand to have a cup of coffee. (Research has shown that the caffeine present in coffee and cola often helps in telepathic communication.) Keep your eyes closed most of the time, and put yourself in a relaxed and passive attitude. (In the course of your experiments, it would be helpful, too, if you experiment with various objects.)

HOW TO CONSTRUCT A MENTAL EARPHONE
(Or Tele-Receiver)

Here is another powerful secret which you may use if you wish to read your friend's mind at a distance. It is a Mental Earphone or Tele-Receiver that will help draw his thoughts to you. The main principle of the Tele-Receiver is that it helps your "inner ear" concentrate by removing all outside distractions.

There are several ways to make or use such an earphone, ranging from a simple use of your hand to an actual earphone (such as the kind used to monitor telephone conversations).

The first of these methods requires complete silence and involves the use of your hand. Cup your hand to your ear, resting the edge or base of your palm against your cheek or jaw. Keep your thumb away from you. Rest your fingers above your ear, against the side of your head. Arch the body of your hand so that it never touches your ear.

Tilt your head slightly in the direction in which you are listening. Now think of the person whose mind you are trying to read. Picture him as situated wherever he is likely to be. Try to get the "feel" of this person's personality, as mentioned before: how he walks and talks, his likes and dislikes, his temperament, how he reacts to different situations, what he's likely to be thinking about at this moment.

The purpose of your hand is to increase the flow of electricity to your brain. As was stated earlier, your body is filled with electricity, which may be channeled to and from the body, or to any part of the body desired. Electricity, for example, is created by the friction of your blood running through arteries and veins. The electricity so generated can be channeled, through your fingers, to enter whatever is touched.

By concentrating on your friend's voice, for example, a thought current is set up in your brain. It is of exactly the same wave length and frequency as the thought in your friend's mind. By placing your hand to your ear, near the auditory nerve, you sensitize and increase the power of your "inner ear" to "hear" this wave frequency, which is then translated into the actual thoughts of the person whose mind you are reading.

The thought currents emanating from your friend's mind, wherever he is, might be compared to the ripple set off by a pebble thrown into water, making larger and larger circles. That is what radio waves look like, and it is no more remarkable that you should be able to pick up your friend's thought waves, out of thousand of others, than it is for your radio to pick up one station out of thousands and thousands that are sending radio signals into the atmosphere.

More important than anything I could say describing this technique is the simple fact that it works. But it requires *concentration*—the concentration of your "inner mind."

Another way to achieve such concentration is to "lull" your outer ear into a sort of slumber or light trance, walling out outside noises and distractions. This enables the inner ear to concentrate and attune itself to the thoughts of the person whose mind you wish to read. (The trance, by the way, can be broken at any time, simply by shifting your eyes or moving your body in some way.)

To do this, the outer ear is deliberately fixed on, or fascinated by some steady sound or beat, such as the sound of boiling water, steam, or a running faucet.

An actual Mental Earphone may be used for this purpose, any object or instrument that will make a steady droning or humming sound.

Any hollow object that you can hold to your ear will do, such as a seashell, a paper cup, an ordinary drinking glass, teacup, or round, bowl-shaped ashtray. A piece of hollow rubber tubing would be excellent. A somewhat fainter sound may be obtained by holding one or both hands to your ears.

As you can see, no wires, batteries, or motors are necessary. To produce the steady "hollow" sound, the object should have some indentations (such as an ashtray) or ruffles (such as a seashell), or be held lightly to the ear (glass or cup). (The end of a tube that is open at both ends should be held as firmly as possible to the ear.)

If you wish, you may use a more sophisticated instrument that produces a droning sound. Some radios and TV's, as well as tape recorders and some walkie-talkies, purr or hum between stations or when the motor is just running. Many of these come equipped with earphones the size of a hearing aid or larger with which this sound may also be heard.

Other items that may be used to produce a droning sound are an electric shaver; a wall or table fan; a small hand-held battery-powered fan; a kitchen blender or mixer (with blades removed); a wristwatch that ticks steadily, or a kitchen wall clock whose electric motor may be heard humming.

When you find yourself comfortably concentrating on this sound, you will be able to shift your "inner mind" to the contemplation of your friend, as described before. His or her thoughts should soon come to you with unmistakable clarity.

OVERHEARS CONVERSATION WITH MENTAL EARPHONE

In his book, *Enigmas of Psychical Research,** James Hyslop reports the following experience of a beginner with the Mental Earphone:

* James Hyslop, *Enigmas of Psychical Research* (Boston, Mass.: Herbert B. Turner & Co., 1906).

"Miss G. F. had been experimenting with a friend for telepathy. Some time after he had left, she picked up her shell and held it to her ear. The conversation which they had had at the experiments was repeated in an aural hallucination, and in the midst of it came the . . . words: 'Are you a vegetarian, then?' Miss G. F. at once wrote to her friend, stating the facts, and asked him if he was responsible for this (fragmentary message). He replied that about fifteen minutes after he had left her he met a friend who made some allusions to a vegetarian restaurant, and that he, Miss G. F.'s friend, had interrupted him with the question: 'Are you a vegetarian, then?' "

THE AMAZING POWER YOU NOW POSSESS

When you have followed the steps outlined for you in this book, you will be in a position of great advantage over others. With the Mental Earphone, for example, you will find that you can actually hear the unspoken thoughts of any person who happens to be standing near you, and that you can even tune in on these people at a distance of many miles, if you so choose.

> You may find yourself standing next to someone in the supermarket, for example, looking at his silent, smiling face—and *hear* him thinking about what a fine day it is, how he would like to go bowling, or any number of things. At first, you may catch just a word, or several words. But as your Telecult Power develops, you will find that you can easily "read" complete thoughts.

Used wisely, this power can aid you enormously. Ever wonder, for example, when making an important purchase, such as a house, a car, or expensive furnishings, whether you were being cheated, overcharged, or stuck with a lemon? Mind Reading can be your insurance against being taken advantage of.

The Mental Earphone has helped countless young people

find and marry their perfect mates. Young women find it a help in judging their boy friends (and the opposite is also true).

In one instance, the Mental Earphone revealed the culprits in an office plot to the man who was being victimized by their scheming. In another case, the Mental Earphone revealed the exact location of a child who was locked in a department store after closing time by accident, and who was pleading for help.

Your Mental Earphone can reveal business plans and opportunities long before they are announced. Many a low-paid worker has risen to wealth simply by "tuning in" on the minds of his bosses and superiors with Telecult Power. Taking an example from my own personal experience, I was able to double my salary and get rapid promotions with practically no effort at all, simply by tuning in on my bosses' minds, finding out what needed to be done—as well as *how* to do it—long before anything was mentioned. In this manner, it *seemed* that I was smarter and harder working than those around me, when actually I was not. And so I was praised and rewarded.

HOW TO MAKE MONEY EASILY WITH YOUR MENTAL EARPHONE

I know real estate salesmen, department store clerks, gas station attendants, even Fuller-Brush men who have doubled, tripled and quadrupled their salaries—and in some instances, have even become partners with their bosses, or have eventually taken over the business—with this Mental Earphone.

I know many small shopkeepers, for example, who, by using this power to "tune in" on the minds of customers, have been able to stock up on fast-moving products and sell them at a great rate; who, by reading people's minds, have been able to find out what they like to talk about, what moods they are in, so that these people come back time after time—*and bring their friends*—simply because they like these shopkeepers, who always seem to know how to please them. As a result, what was a small, hole-in-the-wall, shoestring operation, rapidly blossomed into a large, thriving business—in every single case.

YOUR POT OF GOLD

Even more startling, it is possible for anyone, using the Mental Earphone, to "tune in" on the Mass Mind (the minds of thousands of people at once), through Deep Relaxation, to discover gold-mine opportunities: single, small desires—such as a way of saving time or money when shopping, a desire for a new fad which is rising up in people's minds (like the comeback of an old style of clothing or entertainment, or a status symbol that is striking many people's fancy)—and many other desires which, if shared by enough people, need only be offered to them by *you* to make you a fortune.

To tap the Mass Mind for such information, all you need do is follow the procedure for Deep Relaxation given in this chapter, *willing* beforehand that your mind will be attuned to the general desires of the mass of humanity around you. The strongest impressions you receive, those that arise time and again during your Deep Relaxation sessions, are the ones that will be the news of tomorrow! Money-making ideas that you can cash in on *now* by planning your strategy, by finding a way to provide the product or service cheaply, by stocking up on an item (if it is already in existence) *now*, while you may still do so cheaply before there is a run on the market for it!

HOW TO MAKE MONEY WITHOUT WORKING

Fortunes have been made on the stock market with this technique. You might discover a mass desire, for example, like the "sudden" rush to buy compact cars a few years ago; then buy stock in a car company while the price is low. I know a man who regularly makes thousands of dollars a week this way, without lifting a finger! Another who built a retirement fund of $500,000 in just a few years. And still another, a man in his sixties, who made $9,000 in three months, using this technique. Yet every one of these people—and many more, including housewives, retirees and others who have made money by leaps and bounds with Telecult Power—swears that he does not know a single thing about "high finance"!

But that's the least of it! For by tapping the Mass Mind, as shown in this chapter, the *entire plan* for a fabulous new money-making idea may be layed out before you!

A striking example of this is the early automobile. Did Henry Ford actually conceive of the notion of a cheap, horseless carriage and a way to mass produce it all by himself? Or did he, in fact, simply tap the Mass Mind through Telecult Power? Many think he did, for at the time several prominent inventors were working on the same idea in strictest secrecy.

HOW THE MENTAL EARPHONE CAN HELP SMOOTH OVER PERSONAL PROBLEMS

What else can Mind Reading do for you? Last but not least, it can help you in your personal life. For example, say you have a troubled friend or neighbor: by reading his mind, you will know the nature of his problems and be able to exercise sympathy and understanding. What might otherwise have appeared to be rudeness or thoughtlessness on this person's part, you will then understand to be deep thought. You will understand why, perhaps, he forgot to say good morning, was curt or gruff with you, and you will not be offended.

The Mental Earphone can also help you understand a wife, a husband, a son or daughter better. Teenagers, especially, will benefit by your understanding at a time in their lives when they are apt to feel lonely and confused and have a hard time expressing themselves openly. It can help you mend a troubled marriage, strengthen and unite all family ties.

• • •

With the passage of time, your Mental Earphone will cease to be a novelty and become a very handy tool that you can use to good advantage, one that you can "turn on or off" at will. But in order to keep this power, it is necessary to use it.

Keep practicing, every chance you get: at the supermarket, the gas station, at work, or during lunchtime. Use it without shame, for it is a God-given power that was meant to help us, not hurt us—to help us live more easily. And it is a power that money cannot buy, simply because you already possess it.

SUMMARY OF TELECULT POWER #1

1. Thoughts do not need to be spoken in order to be heard.
2. Sound can be sent out in the form of subvocalization (slight vibrations of the throat, altered by movements of the tongue), which can be picked up by a psychic or sensitive person.
3. Sound can also be produced by the human mind itself—sound in its embryo stage—and transmitted via the auditory nerve to the atmosphere around us.
4. You can prove that the human mind can produce sound, merely by listening to your own thoughts. In this case, your ear receives sound from inside rather than outside.
5. Scientists have proven that the human mind can produce sound. They have found that spoken words and other sounds are *faithfully reproduced* when electrodes are placed upon the auditory nerve and connected with a telephone receiver or loud speaker.
6. Your cerebral equipment is amazingly like that of early radio sets. The entire surface of the brain is covered with hairy filaments called dendrites—which seem to have evolved purposely to furnish fine conducting filaments like those of early radio sets. The end point of each of these "hairs" is as susceptible as a lightning rod to all electrical charges near it.

7. The sound issuing from the sender does not have to be audible. It can be many decibels above human hearing, like radio waves before they reach your radio set.
8. Genuine mind-reading demonstrations can be duplicated by anyone who knows how. Since this book shows you how, it is, in a sense, a kind of stage course in mind reading.
9. In a sense, the power which you and I and everyone possess to "hear" what other people are thinking may be described as or compared with an earphone—a Mental Earphone which you can carry around with you. Once you have learned how to use this Earphone, you may use it to great personal advantage.
10. To use your Mental Earphone, it is necessary to practice Deep Relaxation. In Deep Relaxation, it's not that your thinking is different—it's that it practically ceases. Being completely relaxed and detached, you become like a hollow tube through which the message flows.
11. To practice Deep Relaxation, follow the three steps given in this chapter.
12. Having learned how to keep the body subdued and the mind as free of thoughts as possible, it is necessary to sensitize the mind and body, to practice recognizing mental and physical impressions other than your own. One of the ways to develop this heightened sensitivity is through Contact Telepathy.
13. Another method is to practice the perception of subvocalized sound, explained in the section on "Receiving Thoughts Through Space."
14. In reading the mind of a friend, as a general rule, try to think of all the qualities which he or she possesses.
15. If you are standing face to face with the person, look at this person intently, from time to time, without making him feel uncomfortable. Try to get the "feel" of this person's personality, how he walks, talks and moves, his likes and dislikes, his temperament. Finally, when you are completely

"attuned" to this person, relax, and you will find, to your amazement *that the thoughts come.*

16. Secondly, when attempting to read anyone's mind, always wait for those times when he or she seems most relaxed and "at ease with the world." (You will find that the thoughts of others come to you with greatest clarity at those times when both you and the other person are in a good mood.)
17. When practicing long-distance telepathy, if you are a beginner, plan to practice in the early morning, late afternoon, or at night. The atmosphere around you is clearest at these times, free of radio waves and sunspot ions that might interfere.
18. You should especially practice receiving thoughts at dawn or earlier, since everyone's mind, including your own, is most relaxed at that time.
19. If you can manage, obtain some bit of material which has been in close contact with the person whose mind you wish to read. Such an object constitutes an actual link between minds across space, like a "homemade" antenna that picks up thoughts.
20. Do not practice receiving while lying down or tired, lest you drowse. If you feel you may be tired at the appointed time, allow yourself a few minutes beforehand to have a cup of coffee. (Research has shown that the caffeine present in coffee and cola often helps in telepathic communication.)
21. When you have followed the steps outlined for you in this chapter, you will be in a position of great advantage in dealings with others. Mind Reading and the Mental Earphone will be your insurance against being taken advantage of. It can reveal business plans and opportunities long before they are announced, giving you an opportunity to "get in on the ground floor." And it can help you smooth over personal affairs.

TELECULT POWER #2

YOUR PSYCHIC TELE-VIEWER:

How to See Beyond Walls and to Great Distances

"I looked in my crystal and saw Mr. B. . . . hunting for a paper in the drawers of a writing table. He used a particular pen, which I described, and with his hands ruffled his hair till it stood up in a kind of halo. A lady came in and pointed to his hair and laughed. All this was found to be correct. He had been looking for a paper which he wanted to send by post. And his sister (whom I had never seen, and did not know she lived with him) had entered the room and pointed, laughing, to his hair, just as I had seen."—Mrs. Goodrich-Freer, in *Enigmas of Psychical Research,* by James Hyslop (Herbert B. Turner & Co., Boston, Mass., 1906).

* * *

This is Telecult Vision. It includes all psychic visual experiences beyond the range of normal sight, including clairvoyance (the power to see over great distances), x ray vision (the power to see through barriers, such as locked steel boxes, solid brick walls, and sealed envelopes), and thought transference (the power to see what another person is thinking or seeing).

It may surprise you to learn that you have already covered some of the steps necessary to enjoy this power, if you have read (and practiced) the steps in the preceding section on Telecult Hearing. The main feature that both of these techniques have in common is that a mental impression (in this case, visual) is received.

For example, one of the techniques of Telecult Hearing—receiving thoughts through touch—can also transmit visual impressions. As an illustration of this, Peter Hurkos says: "When I shake hands with a stranger, I know immediately his character, his private life, even the house in which he lives. I receive a series of images like those thrown on a screen by a film projector."

THE HIDDEN ANTENNAE THAT YOU WERE BORN WITH AND THE HUMAN TELEVISION SCREEN

In normally sighted people (whether they wear glasses or not) it is the optic nerves that contribute in large measure to the phenomenon of Telecult Vision.

Each optic nerve is not just a nerve, but rather like a horn or antenna that extends from your brain to your eyes. (See Figure A.) It consists of gathered nerve fibers from different parts of your brain. And your retina (back of the eye) to which your optic nerve leads, is unlike any other sense organ. According to the best known anatomists, it is almost exactly like a television screen. (See Figure B.)

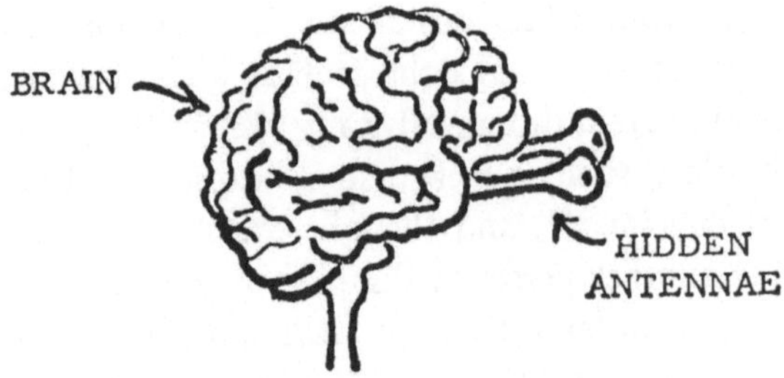

Figure A.

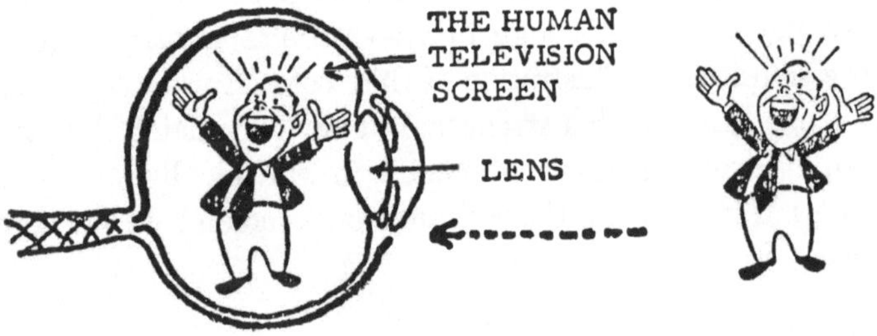

Figure B.

HOW VISUAL IMPRESSIONS ARE RECEIVED ASTRALLY

Some of the fibers of your optic nerves lead from your eyes directly into your brain. This enables you to see. But *some* of these fibers lead from your brain to your eyes, permitting you to *project* thought-forms or mental pictures to your eyes, as in dreaming or daydreaming.

In thought transference, these pictures leave your eyes in the form of nerve electricity, which is nothing but heat. These heat waves are then projected (like a thousand pictures on a strip of film) into the electron atmosphere around us.

They are received by another person in the very form in which they were created; that is, in the form of heat waves. As these heat waves touch the retina (the back of the eye), they are converted into nerve electricity and sent to the visual center of your brain, where they are seen.

THE AMAZING PSYCHIC TELE-VIEWER

With thought transference, actual sights and sounds may be picked up (Telecult Vision and Telecult Hearing) if the person happens to be concentrating on them. In this case, his eyes and ears act somewhat like a television camera that picks up and transmits sight and sound to your television set—your mental television set, or Psychic Tele-Viewer.

And when you "tune in" on someone, you see what he sees, hear what he hears—be it a letter, a picture, some physical object or scene before him (as in a game of cards). It is best to exercise great discretion, if you should find yourself receiving such transmissions, as they may be of a personal nature. When this happens, it is best to "tune off," merely by thinking of something else, directing your attention elsewhere. If you do not, then the next time you meet him you are apt to "slip" and mention something you have "seen" or "heard." This may greatly annoy him, and may even cost you his friendship. But, as I say, if you do not abuse this power, you will not be abused by it.

HOW TO TUNE THE PICTURE ON YOUR PSYCHIC TELE-VIEWER

In Telecult Vision, the actual mental picture of what another person is thinking is received by you. Since most people think in a combination of words and pictures, often the mental picture you receive will include initials, written words, or numerals, like captions on a television picture.

These "psychic" picture captions usually include such information as names of people and places, birth dates, and ages of people involved. These are written, generally, in no particular order across the screen of your mind.

Figure C.

To practice tuning in on people's thoughts, proceed as follows:

STEP ONE

Look up, close your eyes, and stare at the patterns you see (called *hypnogogic images*, or "pictures" on the back of the eyelids). If you see nothing, shut your eyes as tightly as you can for as long as possible and study the patterns before you. Like a child watching a cloud formation, use your imagination to decide what it is and what it may mean. Form your thoughts into words, preferably spoken aloud, and as you vocalize them, your image will tend to focus itself and confirm the accuracy of your speculation.

STEP TWO

Soon you will find yourself sliding into a kind of dream-like reverie, during which the mind may be focused on any person, place or event desired. This is light self-hypnosis that can be shaken off quite easily with any sudden movement of the body.

In this state, you are vaguely aware of such things as street sounds, a dripping faucet perhaps, the ticking of a clock, but they do not bother you. Afterwards, you will feel more completely relaxed and invigorated than if you had just had eight hours of sleep (which is why some people call it "Quick-sleep"). What you are really doing, however, is awakening Telecult Vision.

STEP THREE

It is now that your Third Eye—or mind's eye—may be focused on that which you wish to see. When this happens, think of the person whose mind you wish to read. Picture him as situated wherever he is likely to be—seated at his desk at the office, or at home in his living room watching television, or doing some chore. Focus your attention on him or her.

It is now possible to determine your friend's thinking on any given matter. Relax deeply, with your eyes closed, allowing your mind to fix—if you feel the need of focusing your attention on something—on the mental image of your friend in his surroundings.

STEP FOUR

If it is possible for you to obtain a fresh or recent photograph of your friend in home or office, it is permissible to refresh your memory every now and then by glancing at it, and then closing your eyes.

In view of the radiation qualities of such a photograph (see preceding chapter), it is best to hold it in your hand at all times during the experiment. The fresher and more recent the photograph, the better, which is why I recommend that you take or use a Polaroid shot.

If you have no such photograph, but still wish to enhance your chances of contact, use some other simple object that has been in close contact with your friend's body (and preferably no one else's), or some object that he or she looks at frequently (see preceding chapter, "A Homemade Antenna That Picks Up Thoughts").

STEP FIVE

Perhaps most important of all, make every effort to pick a time when you feel your friend is probably most relaxed or in a good mood. From a distance, of course, it is not always possible for you to be absolutely certain of this. Nevertheless, there are many ways for you to determine his or her probable mood; a telephone conversation at some point during the day, perhaps, or the mood of the person when last you saw him (at work, for example).

• • •

The purpose of this technique is to attune you to another person's mind at a distance. Frequent practice will reveal many facts about this person to you. Once you have succeeded in actually "reading" someone's mind, it will be much easier for you to pick up his or her thoughts in the future, no matter where you are, no matter how great the distance that separates you—though it be across a room, a city, or a continent—even through walls and actual physical barriers.

NOTE: If you should receive a hearing impression instead of

a mental picture, this is good too, although it is not exactly what we are looking for at this stage. Ideally, you should receive both sight and sound. One should never strive too hard, however. If you receive one kind of impression consistently, accept it gratefully and leave it at that.

HE READS MINDS WITH A PSYCHIC TELE-VIEWER

As an example of how the Psychic Tele-Viewer works in actual practice, Arthur H., a carpenter by trade, who uses it as a hobby, recently reported how he used it to read the mind of a complete stranger. With this method, he "saw" that the man had certain photographs concealed in his wallet, which he was able to describe in complete detail. He "read" a letter which was tucked inside the stranger's pocket, tastefully omitting some intimate details, to the genuine amusement of interested onlookers.

And he described many other names, places, dates and events —in exact detail—all of which proved to be true.

HOW TO MAKE AND USE A PSYCHIC TELE-VIEWER (Tele-Photo Transmitter)

Here is a method recommended by L. W. de Laurence, in his book, *India's Hood Unveiled,** to increase the power of Telecult Vision.

Get a small quantity of printing ink—say five drops—mix it well with two drops of turpentine; then put the paste on a piece of glass (a mirror will do), or on a green leaf (maple leaf preferred), making a circle about one-eighth of an inch wide.

Take this device into a quiet room; light a single lamp of low voltage; keep it on a raised level on the northern side of your seat, so that the reflection may come from the north.

* L. W. de Laurence, *India's Hood Unveiled* (Chicago, Ill.: de Laurence, Scott & Co., 1910).

Keep the leaf with the circle of paste in its middle in your left palm and hold it within a distance of one to two feet from the lamp, so that a distinct ray of light may fall on the paste. Then attain a state of passivity by relaxing your mind and body and gaze intently at the reflection created on the paste.

After a short time, small luminous circles will appear and gradually develop into bigger ones; some shape or figure will burst in. If you continue to look at it, these forms will take a definite course. By continuous practice, past and present events will be clearly depicted and enacted before you. When you attain this state at will, command any scene or scenes which might have occurred in the past or may occur in the future to appear. "By the aid of this (method) hidden treasure, lost property, murders, crimes, robberies, etc., can be easily discovered," says Dr. de Laurence.

* * *

It should be noted, by the way, that in all the steps given thus far, mental impressions ("sights" and "sounds") were received from another person's mind. In many of the steps that follow, the same will be true. Indeed, most of the Extra Sensory Perception that is employed by those who know how to use it makes use of other people's minds—even people who are not known to the receiver, since the higher mind eventually develops to the point where it is sensitized to all minds, everywhere (the Mass Mind, mentioned in the preceding chapter).

Thus, if you are able to "see" something in someone's pocket—called x ray vision—what you may really be doing is reading the mind of the person, who obviously knows what's in his pocket. Similarly, if you are able to see or hear clearly (clairvoyance) what is going on in another room or another city, what you may really be doing is using the minds of those present as though they were television cameras (or microphones) transmitting to you.

But it is important for you to realize that Telecult Power need not stop with the use of other people's minds. You have a third or inner eye, capable of perceiving visual impressions directly. No one need send these pictures to you for the simple reason that all objects constantly send out radiations (vibrating, electromagnetically charged particles) in their exact shape. (See Figure D.)

Figure D.

These vibrating particles are actually electrons (the tiniest element known). Everything that exists consists of electrons, which tend to group together with varying density. The denser (or thicker) they get, the more visible they become. For example, everyone knows that a rock or a door appears to be solid, but scientists know that they are just masses of vibrating electrons. These electrons set other particles nearby in motion, and an electrical image of the rock is formed—in fact, many images of the rock are formed, radiating in all directions. (These images remain in the air after the original object is destroyed, which is why Ted Serios can record on film his perception of buildings he has never seen which were torn down long ago.)

PSYCHIC TELE-VIEWER LOCATES LARGE SUM OF MONEY

In his book *Modern Spiritualism,** Frank Podmore narrates a well-supported case in which Telecult Vision was used like a compass to find the sum of "650 pounds of money" that had disappeared. An empty envelope which had contained the money was put into the clairvoyant's hand. (As you'll recall, in Telecult Power #1, such an object acts as a kind of invisible link between itself and anything that has been near it.) The clairvoyant soon saw that the two bank notes and a bill of exchange had been handed in at a bank and that they would be found in an envelope with other papers, in an inner room at the bank. These documents *were* subsequently found amongst some old papers on the mantelpiece in the manager's private room!

PSYCHIC TELE-VIEWER FINDS JEWELED BROOCH

In his book, *My Occult Diary,*† Cornelius Tabori tells how Telecult Vision was used, again like a compass, to find a jewel which had been lost by a Mrs. Kalman. Since Telecult Vision is a power that can be used by anyone who *believes* absolutely and completely in its existence, and since hypnotism is a state of heightened suggestibility, a young man was hypnotized for the purpose of finding this jewel. He was "sent back" to the time and place where Mrs. Kalman had been shortly before her loss. In this state, the young man described how Mrs. Kalman had inadvertently knocked the brooch off while brushing away a fly, how it had been picked up by a dachshund and buried in the garden of the house where it had been lost. By means of this information, the jewel was recovered three days later.

---

* Reported by James Hyslop, in *Enigmas of Psychical Research* (Boston, Mass.: Herbert B. Turner & Co., 1906).

† *Ibid.*

PSYCHIC TELE-VIEWER REVEALS DANGER

The literature is full of cases of hypnotically induced mental powers. In the famous Janet-Gibert experiments, a subject, Madame B., was hypnotized and sent on a "travelling clairvoyance" from Le Havre to Prof. Richet's house in Paris. (Her physical body, of course, remained in Le Havre.) When she claimed to be there she cried out in great agitation: "It is burning! It is burning!" The next day it was found that Prof. Richet's laboratory had in fact been damaged by fire.

PSYCHIC TELE-VIEWER REVEALS WHAT HER FATHER IS READING—SEVERAL HUNDRED MILES AWAY

The well-known Swedish psychotherapist and psychic researcher, John Bjorkhem made similar experiments. In one of them, he "sent" a Lapp girl to describe the scene in her home several hundred miles away. She was able to tell Bjorkhem exactly what her parents were doing, and even what paragraph in the paper her father was reading. This was verified immediately by telephone.

PSYCHIC TELE-VIEWER REVEALS DIPLOMAT'S SECRET

In *A Hypnotist's Case Book,** Alexander Erskine describes how the hypnotized son of a diplomat was able to tell him exactly where his (the boy's) father was, to whom he was speaking, and what their conversation was about. The young man's father bound Erskine never to repeat the experiment.

---

* Reported by James Hyslop in *Enigmas of Psychical Research.*

EVEN THE BLIND CAN ENJOY TELECULT VISION

Since all visual impressions must be transmitted to the visual center of the brain, it is quite possible for blind people to see, provided that there is no brain damage. If, for example, every other means of transmitting visual images to the brain were destroyed, it could still receive them through its visual control center. The brain itself, as we have seen in Telecult Power #1, has billions of microscopic "hair" cells (called fibrils or fibrillae). These cells are extremely sensitive to any and all electrical impressions around them. And they are in constant waving motion, exactly like directional antennae.*

Thus, we have numerous cases on record of people who have been able to see out of the back or top of their heads. The famous German researcher, Dr. Albert von Schrenck-Notzing reported in 1887 how a subject named Lina was able under hypnosis to read books through the top of her head while effectively blindfolded. Perhaps the most famous case of this nature is that of Mollie Fancher.

THE "PEEPING TOM" WHO NEVER LEFT HOME

Mollie Fancher was born in 1848 and lived in the same house for fifty years, some thirty of which were spent in bed after two serious accidents that left her permanently blind and crippled. And yet she could see as clearly as any normal person—clearer, in fact.

Mollie's case was studied by Judge Abram H. Daily, who published a book in 1894 † recounting the many experiences he had had with the woman. A reviewer of the book for the Society for Psychical Research said that Judge Daily had "recorded the

---

* Peter Hurkos believes that the mind is like a photographic plate which records image after image. "What I do is pick up the transmission of these images. I believe everyone has these latent powers," he explains.

† Reported in *The Journal of the Society for Psychical Research*, London, 1894.

narratives of many witnesses whose truthfulness no one would question."

In Judge Daily's book, Mollie's doctor, Dr. Speir makes the following statement: "We have caused a careful and critical examination (of her eyes) to be made by a competent expert —an oculist—and agree with him that she cannot see by the use of her eyes."

Yet she had the power of seeing with a great deal of distinctness, as she put it, out of the top of her head. At one time she did all her work, crocheting, etc. in this manner. She was able to distinguish colors, even to the most delicate shades, not only when absolutely concealed from her normal sight, but while in the pocket of someone who did not know the color of the article to be described. She could read letters placed upon her forehead, or merely by touching them. She could read with many times the rapidity of one reading by eyesight, by running her fingers over the printed pages *in light or darkness.*

She invariably knew what was going on in the room around her and could describe the minutest movements of her guests.

Besides immediate cognition of her surroundings, Mollie's "vision" was able to go beyond the bounds of the room in which she happened to be lying. In this manner, she could "see" the location of lost objects around the house. She was able to "look" around the city and find out what was going on. To Judge Dailey, she once described a man whom she had never met, but whom she had "seen" at the Judge's house a few days before.

Miss Fancher's case of clairvoyance is one of the most thoroughly documented in the history of psychic research. (Hundreds of witnesses saw the feats which she could perform.) But there are numerous cases just like it.

EYELESS SIGHT

Scientists have long known that the entire epidermis or outer skin covering of the body contains photoelectric cells that can transmit actual seeing impressions to the brain. The process of stimulating the skin to the point where it becomes light-sensitive is none other than the basic process of skin sensitization cited in Telecult Power #1 (Contact Telepathy).

Cesare Lombroso, the world-famous psychologist, recorded that he had as a patient an Italian girl who was quite blind but saw as clearly as before, with the tip of her nose and the lobe of her left ear.*

Another case is reported by Professor Carmagnola in the Italian *Journal of Medical Science* † of a young girl, also fourteen as in the Lombroso case, who though blind could see easily with the palms of her hands. In both the aforementioned cases, the subjects could read any printed matter, selected at random.

THE COMPLETE HOME COURSE IN CRYSTAL GAZING

Crystal gazing is another form of Telecult Vision, and the crystal ball a kind of Tele-Viewer, Mirrorscope, or Telephoto Transmitter that helps you concentrate. To quote Frank R. Young, "A crystal ball itself is not necessary, so long as its substitute possesses a shiny surface to stare at. An intensely shiny surface reflects so much light that it temporarily stuns the nerve endings of the optic nerve in your retina so that your eyes perceive only the brightest surfaces within the field of vision and overlook the rest that are darker. The effect partially hypnotizes your conscious and subconscious minds, and your [Inner Eye] then assumes control. . . ." ‡

Crystal gazing is an ancient and widely practiced art. Through its use many strange things have happened. Crimes have been solved, lost articles have been found, hidden facts in the lives of people have been uncovered, and unrealized aspects of one's relationships with others have been revealed.

---

* Hyslop, *Enigmas of Psychical Research.*

† *Ibid.*

‡ Frank R. Young, *Cyclomancy: The Secret of Psychic Power Control* (West Nyack, N.Y.: Parker Publishing Co., Inc., 1966).

Though crystal gazing has been used with some remarkable success in piecing together the facts of the past, its chief use both by professional seers and others is to look into the future and discover what is about to happen or what may happen unless precautions are taken.

HOW THE CRYSTAL BALL—OR MIRRORSCOPE—WORKS!

"I have tried various objects in crystal gazing," writes Mrs. Verrall, in *Enigmas of Psychical Research,** such as cut crystal, a globular crystal, a glass paper-weight, and a glass full of water, and I find no difference in their efficacy. I have also tried under varying conditions of light, with the conclusion that a dim light is the most likely to result in the seeing of a picture.

"I have sometimes seen pictures in quite bright light, but never in absolute darkness. Often I see nothing at all but the bright points of light in the crystal, and often I see nothing in the crystal, but get a mental picture suggesting something I have forgotten to do. Indeed, I find crystal gazing a very convenient way of recalling things forgotten, but in that case I see nothing in the crystal. The difference between a picture in the crystal and a mental picture is quite marked, but difficult to describe; it will perhaps help to show what I mean if I say that the recalled image of what I have seen in the crystal differs as much from the actual image as the mental image of a person differs from the actual person. I believe that with me the crystal picture is built up from bright points in the crystal, as they sometimes enter into it; but the picture, when once produced, has a *reality* which I have never been able to obtain when . . . trying to call up an imaginary scene with my eyes shut.

"It has occasionally happened that I have been able to see more on closer investigation than on the first glance, but if I try to interpose a magnifying glass between my eye and the

* Hyslop.

crystal the picture instantly goes and only recollection remains. The following case is . . . where I have seen a real person, and . . . the picture grew distinct as I looked.

"I saw a black object which defined itself into the head of a man; then I saw that it was my husband's head turned nearly profile toward my left. Behind it was a square-backed chair of brown leather. He was reading, his eyes being on a book, which I could not see. I tried to see the whole figure, in order to know what the book was, and shut my eyes. On opening them I saw the whole figure for a moment, but it was too small for me to distinguish anything."

CRYSTAL GAZING HELPS RECALL FORGOTTEN FACTS

There is an extraordinary phenomenon in psychology called peripheral vision. It means that we see things out of the corners of our eyes without realizing it. (The same thing happens with hearing.) These impressions escape us merely because we were concentrating on something else at the time, but they enter our minds just the same—our subconscious minds—and can be recalled, either accidentally or on purpose. Crystal gazing enables you to do this at will.

Miss Goodrich-Freer gives us some clear examples of this in *Enigmas of Psychical Research.** "I had carelessly destroyed a letter," she writes, "without preserving the address of my correspondent. . . . A very short inspection (of the crystal) supplied me with 'H. House' in grey letters on a white background." She posted her letter to this address and it turned out to be correct.

In another instance she writes: "I saw in the crystal a young girl, an intimate friend, waving to me from her carriage. I observed that her hair, which had hung down her back when I last saw her, was now put up in young lady fashion, the look

* Hyslop.

of which I knew very well. But next day I called on my friend, was reproached by her for not observing her as she passed, and perceived that she had altered her hair in the way which the crystal had shown."

HOW TO MAKE THE CRYSTAL BALL WORK FOR YOU

The first requirement for successful crystal gazing is to relax so thoroughly that your mind becomes a complete blank. Follow the steps for Deep Relaxation given for Telecult Power #1. Without Deep Relaxation one cannot see in the crystal.

The second prerequisite is not to stare at the crystal without blinking. Instead, merely gaze at it calmly and easily. Do not worry about whether you will see anything. Try to think, instead, of what you wish to see. Think about it steadily for a while. Then let your mind go blank. This will seem hard at first, but practice will help you, and practice makes perfect.

Never sit in total darkness, but rather in a dimly-lit room, with the light coming from a window or a low-voltage bulb. The light should be coming from in back of you, never in front. It is best to rest the crystal on a table in a suitable cup or stand. It is also good to cover the table with black cloth beneath the crystal. This helps in concentrating.

There should be no noise in the room. The slightest moving of a chair or loud breathing can distract you and make complete concentration impossible.

Crystal gazing requires much practice. At first you may not succeed. In time, however, you will succeed in visualizing that which you wish to see.

To visualize a specific person, place or thing, picture it as you last remember it, or as you imagine it to be. When you have this mental picture as clear as you can get it, relax completely and deeply. Cease trying to visualize anything and let your mind go blank, like a white screen before the movie starts.

As you gaze in the crystal and your concentration becomes

complete, after a time you will see the crystal becoming cloudy. It will be as if a milky cloud were forming and filling it. This is the sign that the spell is operating.

The final stage is when this cloud-like formation gives way to what you are looking for. Often the picture will be startlingly clear. You will find in the crystal scenes which are meaningful to you. You may see people, houses, places where you have never been, words or sentences, symbols or other objects which have a meaning for you.

If you are giving a reading for someone other than yourself, you should tell only what you see—even if it means nothing to you. Just be a reporter who is perfectly honest. In this way you will build up skill in seeing and describing and very often the other person will supply the missing information or meaning. Do not tell all you see in the crystal if what you see is bad. Practice in crystal gazing will give you a talent which can help in your personal life, and bring a great deal of entertainment to any group (possibly even some extra income).

VISIONS AND "CRYSTAL BALL" PREDICTIONS

There is one class of Telecult Vision for which there are many explanations. And that is *precognition* ("seeing" the future). Is it possible in dreams and visions to "see" the future? Amazingly enough, some persons apparently can do this and, under favorable conditions, it is possible that most people can do it—indeed *do* do it without being conscious of it.

What you may be seeing with Telecult Vision are past events in your own life, or in the lives of others (in which case, you may have read about it somewhere) which were similar in scope and nature to a present situation. Telecult Vision helps bring such forgotten memories to the surface of your mind, as in peripheral vision, mentioned above. Then again your vision may be telepathic.

What you see may actually be future plans in people's minds, received by you telepathically. And finally, your visions of the future may, indeed, be brought on by spirits capable of sensing the shaping up of things and transmitting this knowledge to you.

There is one additional possibility, which is not really prophecy. It is based on a mild form of deception, self-deception really. It is when the prophet doesn't really see the future but thinks he does, or pretends. A suggestion is then planted in the mind of the other person (whose fortune is being told). In other words, it is the power of suggestion working in the individual that makes the fortune come true. Many wonderful deeds have been accomplished—as well as some bad—with this mild form of deception.

DREAM WINNERS AT THE TRACK

One man who used this technique, Michael V., 52, "saw" a horse race at Hialeah. According to the vision, a certain jockey would be riding winners in two races the following Saturday. The vision also told who would place and show. On the day of the races, all horses came in exactly as predicted. The winner of the first race payed $8.60! The next two horses placed and showed at $3.90 and $5.20! In the second race, the winner, a 15-to-1 shot, came in to pay $24.10 at the mutuel window! All this is a matter of record. And Michael V. continued to have similar experiences.

* * *

In another case, an English jockey named Fletcher discovered that he had a tendency to doze off and "see" things. One Sunday, for example, as he waited in a restaurant for lunch, he went into a half doze for a few seconds. What he "saw" was himself wearing the colors of a certain stable, mounted on a black filly, answering the bugle for the fifth race. He "saw" himself pulling up fast on the inside to finish first.

Just then a waiter called him to the phone. It was the owner of this stable, who wanted to know if he would ride a filly named Queen Beauty, a horse rated last in an eight-horse field, at 30-to-1. Fletcher agreed, and bet his full savings, about $400, on Queen Beauty to win. The horse turned out to be the horse of the dream, and Fletcher actually did come in first!

Fletcher's dreams and visions continued. He found that he could deliberately induce a light doze (or trance) merely by closing his eyes and relaxing. In this state he could "see" not only races but other events in the past or future.

SUMMARY OF TELECULT POWER #2

1. Telecult Vision includes all psychic visual experiences beyond the range of normal sight, including clairvoyance (the power to see over great distances), x ray vision (the power to see through barriers, such as locked steel boxes, solid brick walls, and sealed envelopes), and thought transference (the power to see what another person is thinking or seeing).
2. The techniques of Telecult Hearing also prepare you for Telecult Vision.
3. Most human beings are actually born with hidden antennae, somewhat like the story book drawings of Martians, only these are very real. They are your optic nerves. Each optic nerve is not just a nerve, but rather like a horn or antenna that extends from your brain to your eye.
4. Your Mental Television consists of the retina, or back, of each eye, to which your optic nerves lead. According to the best known anatomists, each retina is almost exactly like a television screen.
5. Some of the fibers of your optic nerves lead from your eyes

directly to your brain. This enables you to see. But *some* of these fibers lead from your brain to your eyes, permitting you to *project* thought-forms or mental pictures to your eyes, as in dreaming or daydreaming. In thought transference, these pictures leave your eyes in the form of nerve electricity, which is nothing but heat. These "heat" pictures are imprinted in the atmosphere, like a thousand pictures on a strip of film, where they are seen by psychically sensitive people.

6. When you are "reading" someone's mind, his eyes and ears act like a television camera that picks up and transmits sight and sound to your television set—your mental television, or Psychic Tele-Viewer.
7. Telecult Power need not stop with the use of other people's minds. All objects constantly send out radiations (vibrating, electromagnetically charged particles) in their exact shape, which can be seen by a psychically sensitive person.
8. Crystal gazing is another form of Telecult Vision, and the crystal ball a kind of Tele-Viewer or Telephoto Transmitter that helps you concentrate. A crystal ball itself isn't necessary, so long as its substitute has a shiny surface to stare at. The light refractions temporarily stun the nerve endings of your optic nerves, so that your eyes perceive only the brightest surfaces within the field of vision and overlook the rest which are darker. The effect partially hypnotizes you and puts you in a state of deep relaxation and receptiveness to psychic impressions.

TELECULT POWER #3

HOW TO BROADCAST SILENT COMMANDS—HYPNOSPELLS—THAT MUST BE OBEYED

You have undoubtedly heard of hypnosis and the strange, almost unbelievable power it gives the operator over his subject. Hypno-Telepathy gives you the same power, with this difference: you influence the person silently, by unobserved means.

> **Hypno-Telepathy is based on the proven fact that the human brain can broadcast thoughts to the minds of others—and that, unless you inform the person of what you are doing, he will think your thoughts are his own.**

This phenomenon was discovered as early as 1784 by the Marquis de Puysegur, a pioneer in the field of hypnotism. He wrote of one of the subjects whom he had hypnotized: "There is no need of my speaking to him: I simply think in his presence, and he hears and answers me." Since then it has frequently been found that the hypnotist can communicate with his subject telepathically.

One of the difficulties of hypnotism, however, is that your subject must be convinced of your power, either by your reputation or from what you can demonstrate to him at the time. Also, this person must cooperate with you. Hypno-Telepathy overcomes these difficulties easily.

What's more, this is a power that you can prove to yourself you possess right now.

HOW TO HYPNOTIZE IN 10 SECONDS FLAT!

Before you can hypnotize someone face to face, in 10 seconds flat, you must realize what hypnotism is. Hypnotism is simply suggestion, or the power of suggestion upon the human mind. It is what a person *thinks* is happening to him or around him—apart from, or regardless of, reality.

Any suggestion that you might make to someone else that *he believes,* is a form of hypnotism. If you say something funny, and another person laughs, *that* is a form of hypnotism. In so doing, you suggest or bring a laughable situation to his mind —an idea that *he believes* is funny.

Suggestion need not even be verbal. That is, you need not even speak to make the power of suggestion work for you. Merely by making faces, or groaning, you can suggest laughter, sadness, a pleasant or unpleasant situation. If you do so, and the person who sees you *believes* you, he is in a state of hypnosis. The suggestion may or may not be true, but you have made him think as you wish.

All this can take place in a matter of seconds. Furthermore, emotions—such as anger, grief, suspicion, happiness, or fear—accomplish this much faster. They enable you to force a person to believe what you want him to believe because they cloud the mind to reality. In other words, they enable you to turn his thoughts *inward,* toward himself, so that he cannot see reality.

For example, tell any normal person that he is bright, or handsome, or witty, and he will be greatly taken with this image of himself. In most instances, he will be so busy admiring himself—and thinking that you are admiring him, too—that his mind will be clouded to reality, much as when a person who is busy talking drives his car through a red light, or walks into a telephone pole. He will absent-mindedly agree to things he would not normally agree to—the more so because he is pleased with you for admiring him, and anxious to please you in return. The entire hypnotic process can take place in as little as 10 seconds flat. The aftereffect—that is, the effect of this flattery—lasts much longer.

YOU HAVE FAR GREATER POWERS THAN YOU REALIZE

Returning now to the matter of broadcasting actual complete thoughts, chances are you have already done so many times, without realizing it. For most of us have had brief and often commonplace experiences which can only be explained on the basis of some kind of psychic communication.

For example, you utter a remark at the same time that your companion utters the same remark. You decide to phone a friend whom you have not called in weeks and just as you reach the phone it rings—your friend is calling you. You think of an aunt and wonder why she hasn't written to you for months, so you sit down and write to her; as you are going out to mail your letter the postman hands you a letter from your aunt.

Your dog is lying before the fireplace, apparently asleep, and you think about calling him to come over to your chair. But before you can utter his name he raises his head alertly and obeys your unspoken command.

Or you are suddenly smitten with a vague uneasiness about the welfare of the baby, who is asleep upstairs in a crib. You don't know why, but you just feel that you had better go up and look at the baby. So, feeling a little foolish, you do. Good thing, too—the baby has thrown off all the covers and is lying damply in a draft that blows through the open window.

All this is by way of saying that many of us, perhaps most of us, are far more "psychic" than we realize. Professor William James used to say that we employ only about one-half of our actual powers and capacities in the business of living. This chapter will show you how to control this power and make it work for you all the time. Here are some examples that will show you the power of Hypno-Telepathy.

HE WILLED HER TO DO WHATEVER HE WANTED!

On October 31, 1877, F. W. H. Meyers, of the Committee on Mind Reading of the Society for Psychical Research in London, filed this report on an experiment in mental telepathy:

"I put my hands on M.'s shoulders (Contact Telepathy). I thought of what I wished her to do, and told nobody. . . . I wished her to take a very small ornament from the chimney-piece—a little china cat an inch high. As soon as my hands were off her shoulders she rushed to the chimney-piece . . . and instantly picked up the cat, which was inconspicuously placed among many ornaments.

"I wished her to go to a book of photographs—one of several in the room—open it, and pause at a certain photograph. She rushed quickly to the book (and did so). . . .

"I put my hands on R.'s shoulder (M.'s sister) and willed her to pick up and eat a biscuit from a plate in corner of room. (She did so.)

"I willed her to shake hands with her mother. She rushed to her mother and stroked her hands.

"I willed her to pick up grape from bunch. She rushed to grapes and picked up a few.

"I willed her to pick up a hat in distant part of room. The instant my hands touched her she turned sharply round, rushed to the hat, and picked it up.

"I willed her to nod. She stood still and bent her head.

"I willed her to clap her hands, play a note on the piano write her name, all of which she did."

HOW YOU MAY MAKE YOURSELF TRANSPARENT AND INVISIBLE, BEFORE ASTONISHED ONLOOKERS!

I once had an opportunity to chat with a gentleman who knew a great deal about this sort of power. We were talking about a science-fiction character you may have heard of, who was supposed to be able to make himself invisible, and in this manner solve many mysteries—because he could watch people, without being seen, and likewise listen in on their conversations.

> **I asked him whether such a thing were possible, and when—to my surprise—he answered yes, I asked him if he possessed such power. His only reply was a smile. Pointing to an easy chair in back of me, he asked me to take a seat, so we could chat more comfortably. As I turned to sit down, he was doing likewise. But when I looked up a second later, he had suddenly vanished!**

I instantly jumped up and searched for him, calling out, "Where are you?" I investigated every inch of the room, the patio, the adjoining rooms. There was no trace of him.

Exhausted, I slumped back down on the big leather easy chair, staring blankly at the floor. Suddenly I perceived that my friend was seated in his easy chair, smiling, hands clasped in a contemplative manner.

Had he actually vanished? Not really; but he had, by the exercise of Hypno-Telepathy, obliterated his form so that I could not see him. By directing his thought at me, he had imperceptibly hypnotized me into believing that he would vanish. Following an interval of several minutes, he again directed his thought at me, suggested that I would see him again.

By following the methods outlined for you in this chapter and the next, you ought to be able to do the same! Once you have learned the technique of "silent hypnosis," you may try this vanishing technique yourself!

SHE COULD NOT SEE THE MAN WHO WAS WATCHING HER!

In 1887, the noted German scientist, Dr. Albert von Schrenk-Notzing, tried the following experiment—which you may duplicate—with a subject described only as Lina. It was suggested to Lina that when she awoke from the hypnotic trance she would be unable to see one of the persons present in the room till the word "palm" was spoken.

On awakening Lina repeatedly asked where "Dr. Sch." had gone, though he several times walked past her. Once she actually touched him, and was thoroughly confused by what appeared to be a sensory hallucination. Schrenck passed a full cup of tea to Dr. Sch., and Lina rushed to support it when, as it seemd to her, it was left hanging in the air.*

HOW YOUR THOUGHTS CAN BE RECEIVED BY ANOTHER PERSON

In the chapter on Telecult Vision, in the section that revealed the hidden antennae and television screen that you were born with, you observed that these antennae are, in reality, the two optic nerves that extend from your brain to your eyes.

It is for this reason that your optic nerves can transfer, through your eyes, commands direct from your brain—actually project them outside your body to the hidden antennae (the optic nerves behind the eyes) of another person.

Is this possible, or is it pure speculation? Here are some more facts for you to judge for yourself. It has been determined by the Bell Laboratories that all bodily functions, even the slightest

* Incidentally, many readers will have seen on television subjects who have been hypnotized not to see people who are in the room. The astonishing part of it is that the hypnotized person appears to see what is behind the temporarily invisible person.

degree of thinking, are inevitably accompanied by electric current.

That this current can be transmitted through your eyes to the mind of another person may be proven easily. Just direct your gaze at someone's back, and watch how fast he (or she) turns to you. It's uncanny, but it happens time after time.

If you should have any trouble whatever, this can be easily remedied by focusing at the back of the person's neck, just at the base of the brain. Firmly "will" that he (or she) shall turn and look around, and it will happen!

In the first instance, it was only electric current that reached the other person. This person only "felt" your eyes upon him.

In the second instance, it was something more: *emotions* seem to be able to travel along the electric current that every human being projects, and actually seem to strengthen that current.

But why is it that your thoughts are not more easily received by another person? Because outgoing thoughts—either words or visual images—do have a barrier to overcome, and that is the resistance which they meet at the nerve gaps on their way up and out of the brain.

When your message or command reaches the end of a nerve segment it stops. But the ending of the segment then releases a certain fluid called acetylcholine, which enables the message or command to transfer itself from one nerve segment to the other. (See Figure E.)

This explains why, under ordinary circumstances, the brain emits only very faint electrical waves that are not nearly strong enough to affect another brain, even if only a few feet away.

The reason is that the nerve segment ending has to produce acetylcholine first, before the message or command can be conveyed across the Nerve Gap.

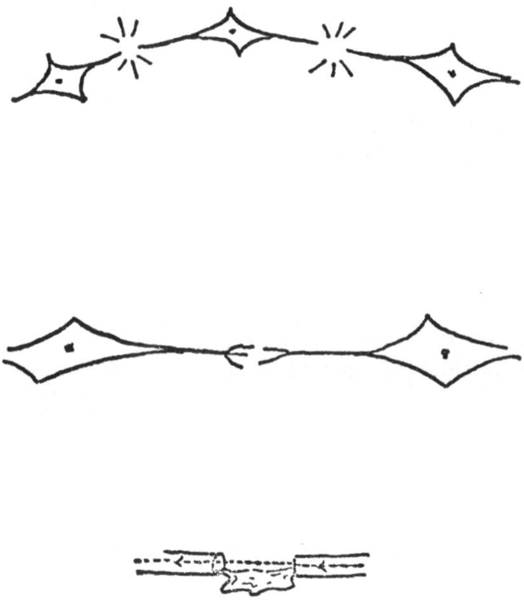

Figure E.

HYPNO-VISION: How to Hypnotize Someone Without His Knowledge

The resistance at the Nerve Gaps can be reduced markedly by giving your brain several consecutive high stimulations. After several such stimulations the Nerve Gaps retain such a large quantity of undissolved acetylcholine that their resistance to the very next message is virtually nil, and the message gets across quite easily. This may be accomplished in either of two ways—through Hypno-Vision, a form of Telecult Vision.

THE FIRST METHOD—Deep Emotion

In many instances of thought reception, an emotional experience of some sort is involved. That is to say, one of the parties concerned is having a frightening, or exciting, or emotionally disturbing experience when his (or her) thought is picked up by another person.

There are innumerable cases on record to support this. In one, for example, a husband claims that three times in his life, he was able to hear—Telepathically—at great distances, his wife's call for help. In every instance, the impression was correct.

The explanation, apparently, is that the receiver somehow tunes in on the emotionalized charge in the other person's mind.

To project thoughts at will, therefore, one method is to produce artificially an emotional buildup before sending. This is a method of thought projection, recommended by Frank R. Young in his book, *Secrets of Personal Psychic Power.**

1. Think of a very pleasant situation, something you like to do, some rare treat—and think of this until your whole mind is filled with the pleasure of it.
2. Think of an even more pleasant situation. Let the thought of it fill your whole mind and dwell on this thought until your entire body glows with the feeling of pleasure and satisfaction you get from this thought.
3. Now, very briefly—for perhaps a few seconds—let your mind dwell on an ordinary, everyday situation; some household chore that must be performed, some tedious not-too-interesting situation.
4. Now, suddenly, just as suddenly as you can, plunge your mind back into that most pleasant of thoughts, and dwell on it again until your whole mind is filled with the pleasure of it.
5. When you have achieved this feeling of intense, sublime pleasure, frame in your mind (either in words or as a mental picture) the situation you wish to bring about involving this person.

* Frank R. Young, *Secrets of Personal Psychic Power* (West Nyack, N.Y.: Parker Publishing Co., Inc., 1967).

It would be helpful if, in this final step, you were looking directly at this person, or in his or her general direction, but this is not absolutely necessary. You may also hold near your body something that belongs to this person, as a means of strengthening contact.

However, these are just additional aids. If you have followed the five steps just given, your thoughts should flow automatically and swiftly to the other person's mind. I tried this method sixteen times one morning, and it worked every time!

THE SECOND METHOD—Deep Concentration

Here's an incredibly simple method that blasts your thought to the mind of the other person with all the power of a lightning bolt. It is called Deep Concentration.

In Deep Concentration, the mind is made to dwell closely, steadily on one thing and one alone. This is not as easy as it sounds. For, left to itself, the human mind tends to flit from subject to subject at a great rate. Try thinking of one single thought for a period of 30 seconds and see what happens.

Here is a method which you may use to improve your powers of Deep Concentration.

HOW TO DIRECT THOUGHTS TO AND FROM YOUR BODY

Direct your attention to the fingers of your right hand. Let the thought of these fingers fill your whole mind. Become aware of every muscle twitch, every throb of blood in these fingers. Concentrate on them. Command them to feel heavy . . . heavy . . . tired. They are the heaviest part of your body, these fingers.

When you have got the feeling, start reversing the process. Draw your thought away from your fingers. Don't look at them, don't think about them. Direct your attention elsewhere. Make believe they don't exist. Think about nothing now, relax. After several minutes, when you pause to check the effectiveness of this technique, you will realize that you have ceased to be aware of the fingers of your right hand.

Now flex the fingers of your hand, and direct your attention to another part of your body. Your nose, for example. You feel the end of your nose quickly enough when a fly lands on it. Make yourself feel it without the fly. Then reverse the process —be aware of no feature of your body at all.

If you've ever felt your ear burning, and remarked, "Someone must be talking about me" (which, incidentally, is probably true), try consciously to make your ear tingle or "burn." Concentrate with all your will power on your ear, until you have achieved the desired result. Then, without rubbing or touching your ear, strive for the opposite effect—no awareness of this part of your body at all.

Now seat yourself in a comfortable position (preferably on the floor, legs crossed) and look steadily at an object directly in your line of vision. Gaze at it naturally, not in an unblinking stare, as this would only prove distracting. Now close your eyes and try to visualize the object in your mind. If the object fades from your mind, open your eyes, refresh your memory, and try again.

• • •

The purpose of these exercises is to help you concentrate on something without being distracted by anything else, such as sights, sounds, memories, even the feel of the clothes on your body. With practice, it becomes easier and easier. Soon you will be able to shut out all unbidden noises and distractions and ignore them completely.

For the sake of simplicity in the pages that follow, I will assume that you have practiced and mastered the second of these two methods, Deep Concentration. As a matter of fact, situations involving Hypno-Telepathy seem to lend themselves more easily to Deep Concentration because, once mastered, it is simpler to use and faster—whereas the first method, Deep Emotion, with its great bolt of power, seems to work better at a distance. (I recommend method #1 in cases at close range when all else has been tried.)

HOW TO BROADCAST SILENT COMMANDS —OR HYPNOSPELLS

Great personal and business success can be obtained through suggestions made to others with Hypno-Telepathy. Suggestions made to others with this method are more powerful than those made through ordinary hypnotism, since there is no need to convince your subject that you, the Hypno-Telepathist, have any special powers. Though preferable, it is not even necessary for you to look at your subject (remember, thoughts project waves like a pebble in the water). And since your thought is transferred directly to his or her mind, you may perform Hypno-Telepathy without uttering a sound.

> **No one can escape the power of suggestion through Hyno-Telepathy. The law is absolute. Everybody, high or low, rich or poor, ignorant or wise, all are subject to its spell.**

In selling, for example, with Hypno-Telepathy, the salesman can actually *make* the customer purchase the article he wants him to. He can actually do the customer's thinking for him, and he will do as the salesman desires. I'm sure that at some time in the past, you have purchased something that you had no use for. This is the principle that was at work, causing you to make the purchase.

HYPNOSPELL #1—HOW TO IMPEL A CUSTOMER TO BUY

For example, say there is a customer in a television and appliance store who wishes to purchase a television set. In front of him is one for $125 and one for $250. A hundred and a quarter is as high as he wishes to go, but there is a salesman standing there, and he is using Hypno-Telepathy on him. Here is what happens.

The customer looks at the more expensive TV and says, "Too bad. It's just what I want but I did not expect to go that high." He looks at the set, admires it, and is undecided about what to do. His mind is passive and is therefore receptive.

The salesman starts by standing in front of the customer and begins to repeat the following words, mentally: "Well, I'll take it anyhow. It's what I want." The customer is passive. The salesman keeps repeating this over and over mentally, while the customer is admiring the set and is undecided.

In a few moments, the customer will blurt out the very words the salesman has been repeating mentally: "Well, I'll take it anyhow." What has happened here is that the salesman has placed himself, so to speak, in the customer's shoes, and made up his mind for him.

You should always use the word *I* when transferring or projecting your thoughts to another person. Never say, "*You* will do this." That is compulsion or force. The person may sense it and resent it. Instead, always place yourself in the other person's shoes, and think the thought as he would think it. Always use the word *I* instead of *you*. No matter what it is you want the other person to do, look directly at him—if at all possible—and silently affirm it as though you were the other person.

HYPNOSPELL #2—HOW TO DOUBLE YOUR FRIENDS AND DOUBLE YOUR MONEY

If you have a small business, and you want to increase your customers, say to each customer, mentally: "I am going to bring you another customer," and visualize it. In a short time, your customers should multiply and keep multiplying. Try it. It works.

HYPNOSPELL #3—HOW TO COMMAND SOMEONE TO SLEEP

In a train, bus, or any public place, select two or three people for this experiment. Gaze at one of them to picture him in your mind. (If you can, without being conspicuous, look directly at him.) Now visualize him doing what you want him to do, and keep repeating mentally, "Deep, deep, asleep." Concentrate all your will power, and believe that this person is going to sleep. Continue to repeat the suggestions mentally. In the beginning of your first few experiments, only one or two of the handful of people you have selected will, indeed, fall asleep. Their eyelids will begin to close, and they will sometimes fight to keep awake, but it is at this time that you must continue to pound the suggestions strongly. If you have followed these instructions carefully, your subject should close his eyes and sleep. Do no more at this time. Your subject will awaken quite naturally in a few minutes. If you wish, you may issue the order to awake ("Wake up!") several times. Rest assured, there is nothing to worry about. This is a good practice exercise.

HYPNOSPELL #4—HOW TO MAKE SOMEONE GET UP AND COME TO YOU

At first, try this with someone who knows your name. Let's assume your name is Tim. Without being conspicuous, look at this person or fix his form in your mind. Then begin the mental suggestions as follows: "Go to Tim (meaning you) . . . Go to Tim . . . Tim . . . Go to Tim." Picture this person getting up and coming over to you (picture it as though this person were looking at you first, thinking about getting up and coming over to you). Say your own name frequently. "Tim . . . Tim . . . Go over and talk with Tim." (Continue to repeat this suggestion mentally, and usually, in a few minutes, the subject begins to make an effort to get out of the chair. At this point, put all the force you can into the suggestion. Finally, the subject will get out of his chair and walk over to you.

If the person is a stranger, or only a slight acquaintance, vary the procedure as follows. Without being conspicuous, look at the person or fix his or her face in your mind. Having done so, you are now mentally attuned. Now begin constantly and continually visualizing yourself as the center of attention with this person looking at you. Imagine this person as thinking that you are handsome and desirable, or beautiful and alluring. Remark on this trait or any other trait you wish this person to notice or imagine about you, saying mentally, for example: "He (meaning you) looks friendly. I'll bet he's an interesting person to talk to."

Remember that this is a stranger you are dealing with, or at best a slight acquaintance. He (or she) may be too shy to strike up a conversation first. If the person does not respond by striking up a conversation with you, the slightest gesture on your part may be all that is necessary—a word, a smile, or a nod.

HYPNOSPELL #5—HOW TO BRING YOUR MATE TO YOU WITHOUT ASKING

In this manner you may also induce your wife or husband or some long admired person of the opposite sex to come to you without asking, be affectionate to you, and voluntarily do the things you have longed for. Simply affirm your desires, beginning with the words, "I want to . . ." or "Let's . . ." as though you were in the other person's shoes, and visualize him or her doing it. The better you know the person, the less time it takes.

HYPNOSPELL #6—HOW TO MAKE SOMEONE TURN RIGHT OR LEFT

While walking down the street, turn your eyes toward any person, whether he is approaching you or walking in front of you, and will firmly that he either turn to the right or left—and you will find that he unconsciously acts according to your orders. This is a good practice exercise.

HYPNOSPELL #7—HOW TO MAKE A FRIEND OR RELATIVE CONTACT YOU

Suppose you wish to contact your friend at a distance. Write out your thought or message on a piece of paper. The message should be a very simple one. Messages easily focused upon include:

Telephone (your name).
Visit (your name).
Write to (your name).

Repeat mentally what you wish this person to do. (Having it written down helps increase your concentration.)

HYPNOSPELL #8—HOW TO INTEREST A TOTAL STRANGER IN YOUR WELL-BEING

Suppose you wish to have an interview with a stranger in order to interest him in your plans or enterprises. To do this it will be necessary to concentrate intensely. Use the method of Deep Concentration given earlier in this chapter. Blank out all thoughts from your mind but one: concentrate intently on the person whom you wish to influence. You may get a mental image of the person. If you have never seen him before, make the mental image without any distinct features. (If you have a letter from this person—even a form-letter from his office—make sure you are holding it at this time.) Repeat mentally what you wish this person to do, and imagine him doing as you wish.

Claude Bristol gives us an example of how this technique is used. In his book, *The Magic of Believing,** he writes of a famous lawyer: "When he dictated he always paced the floor, and his concentration was intense. Once I asked him why he stood while dictating and how it happened that his letters always accomplished the end intended. His reply was:

"'In the first place, I think better on my feet. Then before I start dictating and during the whole period that I talk, I actually visualize before me the person to whom I write the letter. If I do not know him, I try to picture him as I think he may look. In both cases, I direct my thought and words to him in person as though he were actually before me in the flesh and tell him mentally that my premises are right and should be followed by him.'"

HYPNOSPELL #9—HOW TO COMMAND YOURSELF TO HEAL

Your power to influence *yourself*—through suggestion or belief—is called self-hypnotism or autosuggestion. Autosuggestion is, in fact, the basis of all Telecult Power. For without belief in the ability of the human mind to project psychic energy, no psychic, telepathic, or occult phenomena are possible. The very purpose of the true case histories in this book is to help you believe.

For example, if you mentally direct all your attention to some part of your body, that part will soon respond by feeling in-

* Claude Bristol, *The Magic of Believing* (Englewood Cliffs, N.J.: Prentice-Hall, Inc., 1948).

tensely warm or tingly or both. If you have directed all your thought, all your feeling, all your mental energy to that part of your body, your body energy in that area will be increased—and you will *feel* that increased energy.

With this increased energy comes more of everything the afflicted area needs. More blood rushes into and out of the area to carry off poisonous wastes. More antibodies come in with the blood to devour and carry off germs, and eliminate them in the natural way. More of the oxygen, iron, calcium, vitamins, minerals, enzymes and a host of other elements that living tissue needs is brought in to nourish the weakened area.

I am not a doctor, nor do I claim that any of the theories I offer here are palliatives or cure-alls. But they are based on much study and research, the sum and substance of which is this: mental energy directs physical energy. It is a proven fact, for example, that all bodily functions which are not controlled by the conscious mind—such as breathing, heartbeat, eye blinking, and other reflex actions—are controlled by the automatic (also called the autonomic) nervous system. This system runs parallel to and is part of the central nervous system in your spine—*which is an extension and therefore part of your cerebral or mental equipment.*

It is my theory, therefore—and incidentally, a theory shared by many—that since mental energy directs physical energy, cures by mind power ought to be possible. Theoretically, there is only one way to achieve the kind of mind power that brings a healing, and that is through concentration on the desired result.

For those who cannot concentrate sufficiently, there is an easy alternate road, and that is the power of suggestion. For it is a proven fact that repeated suggestion leads to consciousness of a fact, if not belief.

Now, I do not claim that hypnotism or self-hypnotism heals. Not even a physician can claim to do that. He cannot heal the smallest cut on your finger, but the body itself does the healing. All you and I, or a physician, can do, is provide conditions that will assist, or induce, or help the body to heal itself.

But what I do claim, and state flatly here and now is this: mental healing—or Telecult Healing, as I call it—has helped me, my family and others to regain our health. It may do the same for you.

First, see that you are absolutely alone and unobserved. The best time for autosuggestion is early in the morning, when the mind is rested, clear and refreshed. Seat yourself in a comfortable position in an easy chair or prop yourself up with pillows on your bed. Sit quietly and relax all muscles until they are free from nervous tension.

Take the Hypnoscope, a healing symbol, (see Figure F) and hold it at a convenient distance (from 8 to 15 inches) from your eyes; relax, think of nothing. Make your mind as far as possible a complete blank. Do not distract your mind to examine any of the effects you will experience. Keep your eyes fixed steadily on the central white spot of the Hypnoscope.

Now take up the quality you wish to achieve. It does not have to be health. It can be the power to communicate telepathically, to impress a thought on someone. I use health only as an example. Begin your suggestions as follows: "I am perfectly healthy. I can feel as good as I ever did. I am every moment getting stronger and healthier by natural forces. I can and will enjoy absolute health. I have a superabundance of health and vitality in me that will ward off all sickness. I will be healthy." It is not necessary to confine yourself to these words. You may frame your suggestions in any words you wish (a group of such words is called a Photo-Form—see Chapter 7), but they must all be directed toward your single goal.

I wish to state clearly that I do not recommend this method in place of regular medical checkups, especially at the slightest sign of discomfort, but rather as an aid to general mental and physical well-being.

Figure F.

When you have learned to focus your attention, practice thinking along the nerves to a sore throat, sour stomach, or ordinary headache, commanding it to heal and disappear. I have many times repeated to myself dozens of times in a row: "Relax and heal . . . Relax and heal." If you try this, my theory is you supercharge the area with positive energy. The result may come instantly, or even after a few days of accumulated effect.

I have used this method successfully to heal a painful hemorrhoid, an inflamed gallbladder that was causing me a good deal of trouble, and to reduce 50 pounds. In the latter case, using this method, I commanded my mind and body to follow a certain eating schedule—with nothing before or in between meals, although the meals themselves were satisfying, and every lunch and supper contained chocolates, pie or cake. Between September 1, 1962 and Christmas, I shed a total of 40 pounds. By January 1963, I had gone from a hefty 185 to a slim and trim 135. And—rather than gaining back—I retained the weight loss.

Another interesting aside is that, at one point in his life, a friend of mine, a very young man, had tension headaches that were so severe they were literally squeezing the hair out of his head. With this method, his headaches vanished and his hair resumed a luxuriant growth!

In *Reader's Digest* some years ago, it was reported that "Personal worry is one of the principal causes of physical ailments which send people to hospitals. It is literally possible to worry yourself sick. . . ."

In this article, it is stated that "Dr. Loring Swaim, director of a famous clinic in Massachusetts, has under observation 270 cases of arthritis which were cured when they became free from worry, fear, and resentment. He has come to the conclusion after some years that no less than 60% of his cases are caused by emotional conflict." *

The cases are seemingly endless. Telecult Healing can even bring back new youth! Charles Fillmore was nearing the age of fifty, when he wrote: "About three years ago, the belief in old age began to take hold of me. . . . I began to get wrinkled and gray, my knees tottered, and a great weakness came over me. I did not discern the cause at once, but I found in my dreams I was associating with old people. . . .

"I spent hours and hours silently affirming my unity with the infinite energy . . . I went deep down within my body and talked to the inner life centers. I told them with firmness and decision that I would never submit to the old age devil, that I was determined never to give in. Gradually I felt a new life current coming up from the life center. It was a faint little stream at first, and moments went by before I got it to the surface. Now it is growing by leaps and bounds. My cheeks have filled out, the wrinkles and crow's feet are gone, and I actually feel like the boy that I am."

Later, in 1919, at the age of sixty-five, Mr. Fillmore went

* Reported by Claude Bristol, in *The Magic of Believing* (Englewood Cliffs, N.J.: Prentice-Hall, Inc., 1948).

through an illness so serious that those close to him did not see how he could survive. Yet he came out of it with renewed vigor, and lived another thirty years.*

History abounds with many well-authenticated cases of men and women who retained their youth and health in the manner described above, for incredible lengths of time. Among these was Ninon de Lenclos who, when she was 90 years old, was so like a beautiful woman of thirty that a young man barely twenty years of age fell hopelessly in love with her.

And in Pathankot, India, scientific investigators have recently verified the age of Baba Narain Singh as 176, although he gave the appearance of a man in his late thirties or early forties.

HYPNOSPELL #10—HOW TO CONVERT AN ENEMY INTO A LOYAL FRIEND (making someone trust you)

Either look in this person's direction, or fix his image in your mind with your eyes closed, facing his direction if possible. Using the method of placing yourself in the other person's shoes, repeat the following: "I like (your name) . . . (name) is a nice person . . . (name) looks honest . . ." and repeat as often as possible.

Follow it up with many proofs of your sincerity—small favors, honest advice, opinions. Do not overdo it, but try in general to be friendly and dependable. Above all, avoid practical jokes. To test the strength of your telepathic contact, from time to time use Hypnospell #4 ("How to Make Someone Get Up and Come to You").

Other simple ways to test his suggestibility, from time to time, are: hum a tune softly and see if he begins humming. Cough every now and then and see if he starts to do likewise, or clear

---

* *The Household of Faith*, by James Dillet Freeman (reported by Catherine Ponder in *The Dynamic Laws of Healing*, Parker Publishing Co., West Nyack, N.Y., 1966).

his throat. See how enthusiastic he becomes when you describe vividly and in great detail some activity that he enjoys, like baseball or eating delicious food.

HELPING YOURSELF AND OTHERS WITH HYPNO-TELEPATHY

The uses to which Hypno-Telepathy may be put are seemingly endless. It may be used to help both yourself and others. With this psychic instrument, it should be possible for you to help either yourself or a friend . . .

* Get along better with others
* Sleep restfully every night
* Overcome fears
* Lose weight without dieting
* Develop a more powerful memory
* Banish tension and worry
* Improve speaking habits
* Achieve new sexual harmony
* Cut down on smoking and drinking
* Banish unwanted habits
* Increase your powers of concentration

. . . and much more!

Simply apply the same technique outlined so far in this chapter. Remember, when attempting to influence others, always use the first person "I" instead of the word "you" (placing yourself in the other person's shoes)—or use the simple command form, leaving out the word "you." Above all, visualize the situation you wish to occur.

SUMMARY OF TELECULT POWER #3

1. Hypno-Telepathy enables you to influence others by silent, unobserved means.

2. Hypno-Telepathy is based on the proven fact that the human mind can broadcast thoughts to the minds of others.
3. Hypno-Telepathy overcomes the difficulties of ordinary hypnotism, since your subject does not have to be convinced of your power by what you can demonstrate to him at the time.
4. Telecult Power #3 shows you how you can hypnotize in 10 seconds flat!
5. It is not a question of whether you *can* broadcast silent commands—you have already done so many times, without realizing it. This chapter shows you how to control this power and make it work for you all the time.
6. One of the simple ways that you can prove to yourself that you can transfer a command directly from your mind to the mind of another is revealed in the section "How Your Thoughts Can Be Received by Another Person."
7. Another name for this method of broadcasting silent commands—or Hypnospells—is Hypno-Vision.
8. No one can escape the power of suggestion through Hypno-Telepathy. The law is absolute. Everybody, high or low, rich or poor, ignorant or wise, all are subject to its spell.
9. This method may be used to impel a customer to buy; to double your friends and double your money; to command someone to sleep; to make someone get up and come to you; to bring your mate to you without asking; to make a friend or relative contact you; to influence a total stranger and interest him in your well-being; to convert an enemy into a loyal friend; and much more.
10. Hypno-Telepathy may be used for much more than personal profit. It may be used to help others. With this method, it should be possible for you to help a friend: get along better with others, sleep restfully every night, overcome fears, banish tension and worry, improve his or her speech, achieve new sexual harmony, cut down on smoking and drinking, banish unwanted habits, increase his or her powers of concentration.

TELECULT POWER #4

HOW TO HYPNOTIZE AT A DISTANCE WITH THE AMAZING HYPNO-PHONE

As a special aid for contact in Long-Distance Hypnotism, I recommend an amazing hypnotic device—which you can easily make—called a Hypno-Phone. This device, like a magnifying glass, concentrates your thoughts and sends them like a burning streak of lightning to their destination. It is really a *Psychic Tele-Viewer*, one that you hold in your hand, but I prefer to call it a Hypno-Phone, since it is almost like a real one that you talk into mentally!

It is obtained and used in the following manner. Take a large sheet of paper—the dust jacket of this book will do—and roll it in the form of a funnel or cone, big enough to look through the wide end with both your eyes. The inside surface of this funnel should be blank. Any writing or markings should be on the outside. It is a scientific fact that such a device will direct your eyes to the other (narrow) end and restrict your vision to a very small area.

This Psychic Tele-Viewer may now be used as an aid to concentration in the steps for Telecult Vision (see "Crystal Gazing"). Used in this manner, it can help you see and hear beyond barriers such as walls, floors, ceilings and doors . . . locate hidden treasures and large sums of money . . . or actually hear the thoughts of others, since hearing impressions may be received in Psychic Tele-Viewing.

Used in Long-Distance Hypnosis, in 10 seconds the amazing Hypno-Phone should enable you to start broadcasting silent commands (hypnospells) that must be obeyed!

To use it for this purpose, write your message on a piece of white paper. Write or print neatly (not too large) or use a typewriter. Keep the messages short and clear. The one you chose for Hypnospell #7 will do. (As you gain experience, the messages can get longer.) Place the paper with the message before you on a table. Sit near it on a chair and hold the funnel, broad end to your eyes. (See Fig. G.) The whole purpose of the funnel is to shut from your view the surrounding objects and to assist you in the concentration of your vision upon the message. By looking at it constantly you will see the message growing dim and indistinct. But do not allow such a thing to take place; by moving the pupils of the eye to and fro within the range of the paper you can avoid the blurring. In this experiment, the eye should not be allowed to grow fatigued. In case it shows any such fatigue, you should wink your eyes as often as possible. If you practice this exercise daily, your friend will certainly receive your message.

TELEPATHICALLY INDUCED HYPNOSIS

In the annals of clinical psychology at least one case is cited by Gibert and Janet of a subject who could be hypnotized at a distance—*telepathically*. At times she would feel the influence and ward it off by washing her hands in cold water, but in the majority of cases she went into trance without being aware of it. The experiment was carried out by Dr. Pierre Janet and M. Gibert, under the observation of F. W. H. Meyers of the Society for Psychical Research.

Figure G. PSYCHIC TELE-VIEWER or HYPNO-PHONE. Write message on sheet of paper. Then concentrate on message with another sheet of paper, rolled into the shape of a cone, as shown above. This cone-shaped viewer is called a Psychic Tele-Viewer or Hypno-Phone

The results of these experiments are summarized in a table. There were twenty-five experiments in all, of which nineteen (75%) were successes. In one of these experiments, Dr. Gibert actually succeeded in hypnotizing the subject from a distance of three-quarters of a mile, and made her walk through the streets of Le Havre to his house.

GETS RID OF BAD EMPLOYEE THROUGH LONG-DISTANCE HYPNOSIS

"The president of a company that I had been helping was dissatisfied with his sales manager," writes Claude Bristol, in *The Magic of Believing,** "but because of many years of service did not wish to discharge him. 'I was at my wit's end,' he told me, 'when I suddenly got the idea that I could suggest to him

* Claude, Bristol, *The Magic of Believing* (Englewood Cliffs, N.J.: Prentice-Hall, Inc., 1948).

mentally that he ought to resign his job and become a salesman instead of remaining as manager. I thought about it for hours one night, but I nearly fell off my chair when the first thing next morning he came into my office, saying that he would like to resign as manager as he felt that he could make more money by getting out on the street as a salesman. I don't know whether I was guilty of using some sort of magic, but my conscience is clear, because the man today is making twice as much money as he did when he was sales manager, and he's much happier. . . .'"

SALESPEOPLE USE HYPNOSPELLS

Mr. Bristol continues: "A successful book saleswoman told me that if she was satisfied that a customer had the money and really wanted to purchase a book, but was hesitating between two choices, she would keep repeating to herself, but directing her thought to the customer, the title of the one best suited to that customer. She added that many of her sales were made by thought-directive power.

"An automobile executive told me that when he had a prospect who had the money to purchase, he (would always broadcast a silent message to buy) and the prospect did."

TELEPHONE TELEPATHY AND YOUR MENTAL "WALKIE-TALKIE"

In a sense, there are two kinds of telepathy: telephone telepathy, in which the other party is aware that you are sending him a message; and hypnotic telepathy, in which you are sending to an unsuspecting person. Awareness makes all the difference—for without this knowledge, another person will think your thoughts are his own. In both circumstances, the modes of transmission are the same.

If you happen to know someone who can also send and receive thoughts, or if you are willing to teach someone how to do it, then Telecult Power may be used instead of the telephone to communicate with this person.

One easy way to train both your friend and yourself in Telephone Telepathy is with the Hypno-Phone, which becomes a kind of Mental "Walkie-Talkie." After a while, when each of you has acquired the power of concentration necessary to project thoughts without this instrument, you may discard it and send messages to each other in the presence of others without uttering a sound, without anyone being the wiser.

Turn back to the section on "How to Broadcast Silent Commands" (Telecult Power #3) and practice Hypnospells #4, 6, and 7 with a friend, taking turns as sender, with the Hypno-Phone.

When you reach the point where you can both send thoughts clearly, without this instrument, it will be possible for you to hold an actual conversation in the presence of others, without uttering a sound. You may be sitting at your desk in the office, working a machine in a factory, or driving a bus, for example—and be in actual "telephone" contact with a friend or loved one many miles away.

I have used this technique to "speak" to someone in another car, while driving on the highway, instead of a "walkie-talkie." And at work, I am able to speak to someone in another office, without leaving my desk or uttering a sound, and likewise receive answers. I am also able to "tune in" on conversations, although it is a power I use with great discretion.

I know a man who makes a long-distance "call" to his wife * every afternoon, telepathically, to tell her he's on his way home so she can get supper ready. And I know a woman who uses telepathy to keep tabs on her children. The point is, there is

* The members of the Psychodrama Institute of Los Angeles, California, believe that an invisible wire of thought waves connects people who know each other. They believe that when the climate of thinking and feeling in one changes with conscious direction, it also changes in the other person.

nothing difficult about it. You can easily do the same. If you are of average intelligence and no more than average ability, you can send and receive thoughts easily. I have not met one single person who, after a little practice, did not exclaim with surprise and delight: "It works! It really works!"

SPECIAL SECRETS OF LONG-DISTANCE HYPNOSIS

At first, it is a good idea—although not absolutely necessary—to experiment in sending thoughts at only a short distance, perhaps a few feet or less. Experience has shown that the shorter the distance, the greater are the chances of success for a beginner.

Success at a short distance will build your confidence (mainly because you can see the results faster), and confidence is perhaps the most important factor in sending thoughts (the greater your confidence, the greater your ability to concentrate without conflicting thoughts).

In addition, it is wise to follow these basic rules:

1. Never attempt to telepathize to anyone who is in a bad mood; always wait for his or her mood to brighten. Telepathize to anyone who seems calm and contented.
2. Do not telepathize to any person who is engaged in deep thought or heavy mental effort (for example, someone who is engrossed in figuring out his income tax). If you do, your thoughts will never get through. Someone who is engaged in light, routine work, however, is susceptible (for example, someone who performs the same job with a machine all day, a typist or assembly line worker). The more boring, tedious, and obviously uninteresting the work is that the person is engaged in, the more susceptible he is to Hypno-Telepathy (Long-Distance Hypnosis).
3. Beware of involving third parties in uncomplimentary thoughts; they might be brought in tune and receive

more or less accurate impressions with a feeling that you are hostile (the more potent a transmitter you become, the more danger there will be).

4. When you want anything done, don't just ask; *command!* This very state of mind, commanding, is stronger even than words in getting what you want. To command, mentally, requires such strong faith in one's self that the brain power is intensified. To command telepathically, imagine that you are the other person and that you are *ordering* yourself to do something. Mentally shout, "*Go over and chat with Pete* (yourself)" or whatever other command you wish to transmit.
5. Visualize the situation you want to bring about. This means, try to "see it in your mind's eye"; form the most vivid mental picture you can, while commanding the situation to come about. You may keep your eyes closed for this, if you wish.
6. If at all possible, try to face in the general direction of the person or object you wish to influence. Even if that person is on the opposite side of a wall or glass partition. In distance telepathy, and only if you are alone, use the Hypno-Phone.
7. Be as discreet as possible in practicing mental telepathy on others, lest you arouse scoffers. Never let it be known to people around you that you are trying to influence them to do your bidding. Resentment and contrariness would be the natural response you could expect.
8. Do not for one moment doubt that you can send (or receive) thoughts. You *can.* Every human being on the face of the earth who wants to, and is willing to follow these simple instructions, can do it. Faith or confidence is probably the most important factor in sending thoughts.

Yes, in Telecult Power as in everything else, the doubting Thomas is at a disadvantage. "Belief creates its own verification in fact," William James once said. "Only believe, and you shall see," go the words of an old hymn. "Faith can move mountains," says the Bible.

"The doubter will not be able to discover or use his untapped psychic resources until he gives up his doubt," writes Alson J. Smith, "for doubt is the acid that eats away at the foundation of the life of mind and spirit."

Telepathy, and other Telecult phenomena, seem to be based on a positive-negative force of some kind—like electricity—operating on wave lengths yet to be identified. And like electricity, telepathy needs a completed circuit to operate. For example, it has been observed that one skeptical person can frequently interrupt or block a séance. His antagonism acts as a kind of short circuit in the circle of joined hands.

HOW TO PROTECT YOURSELF FROM PSYCHIC ATTACK

Any psychic attacker who wishes you evil can use Telecult Power to make your suffer. You are especially vulnerable if you are the sensitive type. If you are, you cannot help but suffer from slights and insults and unfriendly thought messages from people who dislike you.

When you sense that you are under psychic attack, there is only one thing to do. You must develop an immediate psychic block or "shield" to prevent the other person's thoughts from implanting themselves in your mind.

How does one know when one is under psychic attack? Ask yourself these questions:

* Are you having trouble with your marriage, or are you having other romantic difficulties?
* Did your rival get the promotion you deserved and ex-

pected? Does your boss have a good reason for not giving you a raise?

- Have you recently been plagued by nervousness, fidgeting, or poor health for which your doctor can find no cause?
- Has insomnia replaced eight hours nightly restful sleep?
- Are other people forcing you to pay homage to them, agree with them, do things for them against your will—or making you "look silly" in front of others?

These are a few signs that you may be under psychic attack from a spiteful husband or wife, an exploiting boss, an unfriendly neighbor, a bossy friend, pushy co-workers, or a hidden enemy—perhaps even non-human—all of whom are capable of perpetrating a psychic attack against you.

When you find yourself unconsciously doing something the wrong way, making double work for yourself, purchasing items you don't need, blurting out offensive remarks in public without meaning it, etc., you may reasonably suspect that you are under psychic attack.

HOW TO CREATE A PSYCHIC SHIELD

Among the questions you should ask yourself at this time is, has anybody you know recently said that he hoped you would do any of the things you have done? Suggestion can be a powerful weapon when used against you.

Whether or not the culprit is revealed in this manner, your next step would be to affirm over and over again—as many times as necessary—"I will not receive this person's thoughts." In this way, you create what amounts to a psychic shield that effectively blocks this person's influence from your mind.

Then, using your Hypno-Phone, you immediately begin using Hypnospell #10, "How to Convert a Dreaded Enemy into a Loyal Friend."

When you are confronted face-to-face with an obvious psychic attack, as for example when a fast-talking salesman bombards you with reasons why you should buy his product, or when a belligerent enemy engages in name-calling or sarcasm, you must create what is known as an auditory psychic shield—that is, a shield against hearing his voice.

This is done by immediately thinking of something else—anything—as long as it takes your mind off the attacker's voice. It's easy to do. You can do it right now, to prove it to yourself. Turn on your television set and then go out of the room, so you can still hear it, but not see it. Now take this book and start reading from the beginning of this section, "How to Create a Psychic Shield" to this point. If you have effectively been concentrating on what you are reading, you will suddenly realize that you have not heard one word that was being said on TV.

Another way to avoid psychic attack is to tune in on your friends, from time to time, with any of the thought-receiving techniques mentioned in the first two chapters of this book. If you should discover a hidden enemy this way, repeat over and over, "I will not receive this person's thoughts."

PSYCHIC BACKLASH: WHAT IT IS AND HOW TO AVOID IT

It is a scientific fact that evil has a tendency to backfire, and that the evil you do tends to come back to you. This is the psychic phenomenon of "backlash."

In other words, if you use Telecult Power with evil intent, you may run up against another person who knows how to use it, enabling him to detect you for certain and to retaliate against you.

Another way that any evil schemes you may find yourself contemplating could backfire against you is psychologically. A simple guilt complex may take hold in your mind and grow, causing you to hurt yourself (unconscious punishment) at least as much as the person you wish to hurt. For example, you might find yourself thinking about it so much that your work suffers at the office or factory, and you are reprimanded or even fired.

It is a bad idea, therefore, to use any telecult power with evil intent. Besides the fact that you risk psychic backlash against yourself, there is no need for it. Telecult Power, as normally used in the course of everyday living, provides all the knowledge, all the power, all the safety and ease of living that anyone could possibly desire.

SUMMARY OF TELECULT POWER #4

1. As a special aid for contact in Long-Distance Hypnotism, you can make and use the amazing Hypno-Phone.
2. This device concentrates your thoughts and sends them like a streak of lightning to their destination.
3. Since it is really a Psychic Tele-Viewer, one that you hold in your hand, you may use it as an aid to concentration in Telecult Vision (see Telecult Power #2). Used in this manner, it can help you see and hear beyond barriers such as walls, floors, ceilings and doors.
4. Used in Long-Distance Hypnosis, in 10 seconds the amazing Hypno-Phone should enable you to start broadcasting silent commands (hypnospells) that must be obeyed!
5. In a sense, there are two kinds of telepathy: telephone telepathy, in which the other party is aware that you are sending him a message; and hypnotic telepathy, in which you are sending to an unsuspecting person. Awareness makes all the difference, for without this knowledge, another person thinks your thoughts are his own.
6. Telephone telepathy enables you to speak to someone, in the presence of others, without uttering a sound. If you are of average intelligence, and no more than average ability, you can send and receive thoughts easily.
7. To use your Hypno-Phone, it is a good idea at first to send simple messages at a short distance.

8. Never attempt to telepathize to anyone who is in a bad mood. Always wait for his mood to brighten.
9. Do not telepathize to any person who is engaged in deep thought or heavy mental effort. Someone who is engaged in light, routine work, however, is susceptible. (The more boring, tedious, and obviously uninteresting the work is that the person is engaged in, the more susceptible he is to ypno-Telepathy.)
10. Beware of involving third parties in uncomplimentary thoughts; they might be brought in tune and receive more or less accurate impressions of what you really think of them.
1. When you want anything done, don't just ask, command! To command telepathically, imagine that you are the other person and that you are ordering yourself to do something. Mentally shout, "Go over and chat with Pete (yourself)" or whatever.
12. Visualize the situation you want to bring about.
13. If at all possible, try to face in the general direction of the person you wish to influence.
14. Use the Hypno-Phone only if you are alone.
15. Be as discreet as possible in practicing mental telepathy on others. Never let it be known to people around you that you are trying to influence them to do your bidding. Resentment and contrariness would be the only response you could expect.
16. Do not doubt for one moment that you can send (or receive) thoughts. Every human being on the face of the earth can.
17. Any person who wishes you evil can use Telecult Power to make you suffer.
18. When you sense that you are under psychic attack, there is only one thing to do. You must develop an immediate psychic block or "shield" to prevent the other person's thoughts from implanting themselves in your mind. Follow the in-

structions in the section of this chapter titled, "How to Create a Psychic Shield."

19. It is a scientific fact that evil has a tendency to backfire, and that the evil you do tends to come back to you. This is the phenomenon of "backlash." In other words, if you use Telecult Power with evil intent, you may run up against another person who knows how to use it, or you may develop a simple guilt complex.
20. It is a bad idea, therefore, to use any telecult power with evil intent. Besides the fact that you risk backlash against yourself, there is no need for it. Telecult Power provides all the knowledge, power, safety and ease of living that anyone could possibly desire.

TELECULT POWER #5

YOUR MENTAL LEVITATING FINGER

Further evidence of the power of mind over matter is *telekinesis* (derived from two Greek words meaning "far motion"), the moving or control of objects without touching them.

Telekinesis is a fancy word for something that happens all around us all the time. Another word for it is "remote control." Toy trains, as well as real ones, can be controlled from a distance, without touching them, by means of electrical signals. Spacecraft as well as all manner of cameras and equipment may also be controlled without physical contact and at a distance of hundreds of miles. By means of tiny electrical impulses, directed by a remote control unit which you can hold in your hand, you can turn on a television set at the far corner of a room without leaving your chair, select the program you desire and adjust the controls without actually touching the set. Of course, this form of telekinesis all depends on mechanical equipment. Or does it?

According to those who have tried it, it is possible to achieve the same results without equipment of any kind—through mind power alone, by means of deep concentration and the use of sending techniques similar to those described in Chapter 3. For the human mind produces electrical impulses, too, which can be directed toward any object. Although some people—without ever taking the trouble to investigate the matter—will simply pooh-pooh the idea, this book shows you how, through certain simple techniques, you should be able to increase the power of your brain waves, with a kind of Psychic Tele-Command, direct them toward any object outside your body and move that object, without touching it.

HALTS TRAINS WITH MENTAL LEVITATING FINGER!

In an amazing and true example of Telecult Power, a commuter on the New York subway system reports how every time he enters a terminal and finds the train about to leave, he uses this simple yet staggeringly mighty power.

Instead of missing the train, while he fumbles through his pockets at the toll gate—*now* he merely points his mental levitating finger at the train to stop it, often bringing it to a screeching halt in mid-motion. Onlookers attribute it to some kind of phenomenal luck, or perhaps a friendly conductor or motorman, but this commuter insists it is no such thing.

With this power, he is not only able to stop a train—and prevent it from moving no matter how hard the motorman tries to start, he says, but he is also able to make the doors open, without touching them, much to the engineer's surprise, no doubt.

THE SCIENTIFIC EVIDENCE OF TELEKINESIS

To get clinical data on telekinesis during the last twenty years, many academic, systematic, investigations have been conducted, notably by Professors Joseph Banks Rhine, Oliver Reiser, and Ernest Hunt Wright, at Duke, Pittsburgh, and Columbia Universities respectively. The evidence is overwhelming that human and animal minds send and receive intelligence to and from other minds and *to and from inanimate things.*

> More important is the preponderance of evidence that minds can command actions to be carried out not only by other humans and by animals, but by absolutely lifeless inorganic matter—a pair of marble dice, for example!

Perhaps the most outstanding work in this field has been done at Duke University, where Dr. Rhine and his associates have demonstrated that telekinesis is more than idle theory. Dice were thrown by a mechanical device to eliminate all possibility of trickery. Since 1934 when experiments of this type were started, millions of throws of dice have been made. The results were such as to cause Dr. Rhine to declare that "there is no better explanation than that the subjects influenced the fall of the dice without any recognized physical contacts with them."

By mentally concentrating upon the appearance of certain numbers, while at the same time they stood at a distance to avoid all physical contact with the mechanical thrower and with the dice, the experimenters were frequently able to control the dice. In a number of the experiments, the scores made under telekinesis refuted some of the traditional mathematical odds of a million to one against the reappearance of certain combinations of numbers in repeated succession.

HOW TO USE YOUR MENTAL LEVITATING FINGER

These experiments give you some idea of what is meant by "Thought creates after its kind," "Thought correlates with its object," "Thought magnetically attracts that upon which it is directed," and similar statements that we have heard for years. No matter what the character of the thought, it does create after its kind. In telekinesis, you can prove this to yourself easily enough. For you possess a kind of Mental Levitating Finger that can move objects without touching them, and requires only a little practice to be used. Proceed as follows:

1. Take a piece of medium-weight paper, about three inches square, and fold it diagonally from corner to corner. Then open it and make another diagonal fold so that there will be two folds or creases forming intersecting diagonals. Again open the paper, which will present the appearance of a low, partially flattened-out pyramid. Now take a long needle and force it through a cork so that the point extends an inch or so above the top side of the cork. Place the cork with its needle, point up, on top of an inverted water glass, so that there may be free movement of the paper, which is to revolve on the needle point. Take the piece of paper and balance it, where the creases intersect, on the point of the needle, placing it so that the four sides of the pyramid point downward.

   Place the glass, with the cork, needle and paper on a table or desk. Then place your hands around the piece of paper in a cupping fashion, keeping them a half inch or so away from the paper, so that it may move freely. Now order it to revolve upon the needle point. At first it will wobble—perhaps revolving slowly at first and in one direction or the other; but if your hands remain steady and you concentrate upon a certain direction of movement, the paper will revolve until it turns rapidly upon the needle point. If you mentally order a change in direction, the one-way movement will cease and the paper will start revolving in the opposite direction.

2. Another method is to use a small disc of cardboard known as a "dialette" bearing the facsimile of the face of a clock, with numbers from one to twelve. (This is better known as the Rosicrucian Dialette and is issued by Amorc, Rosicrucian Brotherhood.) A sharp needle is pushed through its center and on top of it is balanced a sliver of thin cardboard fashioned in the shape of an arrow. The disc is placed on top of a glass filled with

water. The operator places his hands around the top of the glass, the disc, and arrow; then orders the arrow to revolve, change its position, or stop at any desired position or number.

3. Get an ordinary pair of dice. Take one of the dice and choose the side you wish to come up. Press this side against the palm of your throwing hand, but do not rub it. Fix the number firmly in your mind, and after a few seconds roll this one dice, willing that number to come up. Make sure, as the dice cube leaves your hand, that your hand remains extended with the fingers stretching outward and the palm facing the dice cube. When you have had a fair number of successes, take both dice in your hand. Choose the sides you wish to come up. (It may be easier at first if you pick the simpler combinations or even numbers, to picture in your mind.) Press the dice, with these sides down, against the palm of your throwing hand. Fix the numbers firmly in your mind, then roll them, willing that combination to come up. Make sure, as the dice leave your hand, that your hand remains extended, palm out. After a few days' practice, you should have extraordinary success.

Practice with larger and larger objects, trying, in turn to influence the path a small animal takes, such as a cat or dog. Try to influence the motion of people's hands or bodies when they move. This may even be tried on a baseball, or the players, when watching such a game. Then try influencing the motion of larger objects, such as automobiles.

In explaining telekinesis (or psychokinesis, as it is also known), Dr. Rhine points out that there must be a mental attitude of expectancy, concentration of thought, and enthusiasm for the desired results if a person is to be successful.

That belief is the basic factor in the ability to demonstrate psychokinesis (control of mind over matter) and telepathy was confirmed in experiments at Duke University as reported in the

New York Herald Tribune by John J. O'Neill. He told of how a young woman, by distracting the attention of one of the young men attempting to control the fall of the dice, and by scoffing at his professed ability to demonstrate his power of mind to direct matter, succeeded in injecting such a negative factor that she weakened his belief in himself and ruined his score. Mr. O'Neill made an interesting speculation about this when he went on to say: "The converse of this experiment, still to be made, in which a test would be made of the possibilities for improving the score by a confidence-inspiring 'pep' talk offers interesting possibilities."

HOW YOUR MENTAL LEVITATING FINGER MAY BE USED IN GAMES OF CHANCE

There are many professional gamblers who contend that a strong mental influence has much to do with achieving so-called lucky results in games of chance, such as card playing, the calling of dice, the operation of a roulette wheel—and even games of skill, such as bowling and golf.

One gambler who consistently wins on pinball machines states: "I never go near one unless I am in the mood for it, and that means that I must be in the frame of mind that I'm going to win. [Again, a kind of Psychic Tele-Command.] I've noticed that if there's the slightest doubt in my mind, I don't win. But I can't recall the time that I didn't get winning numbers when the winning idea was firmly fixed in my mind before I started to play."

If a positive attitude, one of supreme self-confidence, does nothing else, it influences the minds of those around you. Many professional gamblers, as well as people from all walks of life, use this trick to actually enlist the unconscious—and even unwilling—help of others!

For by giving the impression that you can't lose, and by looking and acting as though you are positive of this, others begin to believe it. They begin to feel that they can't win. And whenever your turn comes, they unconsciously help you by believing that you will win. Your mental power is then increased many times over, with not just one mind but many minds concentrating on whatever it takes to bring victory to you!

As an example, there once was a foreman in a lumber camp up North who came to shoot dice every Friday night with the lumberjacks. His luck was phenomenal, but because the men saw that his dice were honest, they always came back for more, hoping to beat him when his luck ran out.

One day, the boss sent word that he wouldn't come if they would send him a dollar apiece to stay away. They all rejected this. So the boss came and made another proposition.

He proposed to let anyone who wanted to, roll for him. The players were delighted with this . . . at first. But as the game progressed they began to notice that no matter how poor a man's luck was, he would *win* when he rolled for the boss. What was the boss's secret? *Confidence*. The idea that he *would* win. It was a kind of Psychic Tele-Command that enabled him to win without touching the dice!

HE ROLLS DICE 50 TIMES WITHOUT MISSING ONCE!

On October 13, 1967, I heard a news item on CBS-TV about a man who had just made enviable use of this Psychic Tele-Command over matter. For the first time in the history of Las Vegas, he rolled the dice 50 times without missing once—and walked away with a half-million dollars, the largest amount ever won in a single game.

* * *

Of course, this book is not written for professional gamblers, but for sincere men and women who wish to succeed in life. The material referring to the games of chance is included only to provide further evidence that with concentrated thought, expectancy, and steadfast belief, we actually set in motion vibratory forces that bring about material manifestations.

HOW OBJECTS CAN BE MOVED WITHOUT TOUCHING THEM

Eusapia Palladino could move objects without touching them, in broad daylight, without any trickery. In 1908, a committee of men known for their skepticism was picked by the British Society for Psychical Research to investigate the claims made about her. Each of these men had exposed many frauds.

They journeyed to this woman's native city of Naples. Their investigation lasted several weeks, and each came away firmly convinced that Eusapia Palladino had the ability to tap a supernormal power. Although she could barely sign her name, this frail-looking woman mystified the most learned men of science, and demonstrated her powers hundreds of times.

With four men holding her arms and legs, she could direct a Psychic Tele-Command to a heavy mahogany dinner table to move around a room. As investigators watched, the table would rise and hover about six inches in the air. A thorough search of the premises revealed no wires or electromagnets. When the woman relaxed and ceased to concentrate, the table would crash to the floor.

• • •

Jack Webber of London, England, could also command objects to move without touching them. One time he was photographed lifting a 40-pound bookcase into the air—without touching it. Some of the books were mysteriously lifted from the table and deposited in the laps of those present. The *London Daily Mirror* published a photo of the bookcase in mid-air and gave a three-column center spread to the story.

HOW TO MAKE FLOWERS AND FRUIT GROW LAVISHLY, WITH YOUR MENTAL LEVITATING FINGER

It is claimed ordinary human mind power (or at least the vibratory influence of sound), when directed at plant life, such as grain, vegetables, flowers, and trees, in Psychic Tele-Command, can make them grow more abundantly.

"A number of years ago," writes Claude Bristol,* "we had an old Swiss gardener who insisted that we replace in our yard a number of small trees and shrubs. At first I couldn't see the reason for digging up the old ones and replanting others, but the old man's insistence prevailed. I observed that in planting them, just after he got the small trees in the soil and covered the roots, he engaged in some sort of audible mumbo jumbo. He did the same with the shrubs. One day, my curiosity piqued, I asked him what he was 'mumbling about' as he placed the trees and shrubs in the ground. He looked at me searchingly for a moment, then said: 'You may not understand, but I'm talking to them, telling them they must live and bloom. It's something I learned when I was a boy from my teacher in the old country, Switzerland. Anything that grows should have encouragement and I'm giving it to them."

Luther Burbank is said to have used the same method. In fact, once he tried a controlled experiment. He planted two groups of seeds. As he tended one group, he would always hum softly or whisper encouraging words for the seeds to grow. The other group was always tended in silence. Both groups received the same amount of watering, the same amount of plant food, and were otherwise tended in the exact same way. The seeds that were tended in silence grew up in a fairly ordinary manner, with a large number of straggly plants, short plants and mal-

---

* Claude Bristol, *The Magic of Believing* (Englewood Cliffs, N.J.: Prentice-Hall, Inc., 1948).

formed ones. But those that were nursed with music and praise grew twice as large and twice as healthy as the first group.

In *Unity Weekly* some years ago, the story was told of a farmer who, when he plowed a field, blessed every seed he put into it, and visualized the abundant harvest it would bring. His neighbors marveled at the size of his crops.

* * *

Now it's your turn. There's not a single psychic or occult wonder in this book that you could not duplicate if you would only give yourself a chance. Start by trying any of these experiments in "mind over matter," then proceed to greater levels of psychic power. The magic word is ***believe***. Believe you can do it and you can!

SUMMARY OF TELECULT POWER #5

1. Your "Mental Levitating Finger" is your power to move or control objects without touching them.
2. Another name for this power is "telekinesis."
3. You can prove that you possess this power with any number of simple devices, such as a dialette, which this chapter shows you how to make, or a pair of dice.
4. To make it work, you must have an attitude of expectancy, concentration of thought, and enthusiasm for the desired result.
5. Your Mental Levitating Finger may be used in games of chance, such as the calling of dice, the operation of a roulette wheel—and even games of skill, such as bowling and golf.
6. It has been said that this same power, when directed at plant life, such as grain, vegetables, flowers, and trees, can make them grow more abundantly.

7. There is not a single psychic or occult wonder in this book that you could not duplicate if you would only give yourself a chance. Start by trying any of these methods, and proceed to greater levels of psychic power. The magic word is *believe.* Believe you can do it and you can.

TELECULT POWER #6

HOW TO JOIN THE HIDDEN BROTHERHOOD AND ENJOY A WONDERFUL NEW LIFE OF MONEY, FRIENDS, AND POWER

In its ability to make things happen, your mind is like a Psychic Generator or Duplicating Machine that turns dreams into solid reality. It is a process that extends all the way from a conceived notion within your mind, to the formation of that idea—out of nothingness—into a solid, tangible fact. And this even applies to material objects, which can be brought into being through mind power alone.

At the De La Warr Laboratories, Oxford, England, radionic cameras have been devised which can even photograph a materializing thought. In the December 1954 issue of *The Ark* * it is stated that when a scientist concentrated on picturing mentally a half-opened penknife, the camera reproduced the concept faithfully. A photograph of tap water in Oxford which had been blessed by a priest showed a white cross superimposed

* *The Ark* (Bulletin of the Catholic Study Circle for Animal Welfare), London, England, December 1954.

on the picture of the water, whereas a matching photograph of unblessed water showed no cross.

Now moving into the realm of actual materialization, we have documented evidence of the ability of the human mind to control body electricity, to use it to affect molecules in the air, to slow down the rate of vibrations of these molecules so that they become visible in the exact replica of an object.

This phenomenon has been seen and photographed many times, and lends credence to the theory of the divinity in man. (This is the theory that your mind is like the Master's Mind in miniature—that you actually carry a small part of God around with you all day.)

SHE CREATED A MAN OF SEEMINGLY SOLID FLESH AND BONE OUT OF THIN AIR!

Some mystics, like Madame Alexandra David-Neel, have actually succeeded in conjuring imaginary beings (thought or Photo Forms) out of thin air. As part of her training to become a Jetsumna, or female lama in Tibet, Mrs. Neel had to meditate in solitude somewhere in the Tibetan mountains for almost a year.

During this time she attempted a strange experiment. For six months, she concentrated on the image of a jolly, fat monk. At the end of that period, *her thought form assumed an existence of its own,* and was seen quite clearly by others who chanced upon her hideout. They, moreover, took the monk to be real! This was no transparent phantom, but a creature of seemingly solid flesh!

THE LAW OF MENTAL ATTRACTION
(Your Mental Money Magnet)

There is a law of Mental Attraction that acts along lines very similar to the action of a giant magnet. That law may be stated as follows:

Not only do you attract thought-vibrations, thought-waves, thought-currents, thought-atmosphere or forms of a harmonious character with your own; you also attract (and are attracted by) the people who send them, people whose interests run along the same general lines as your own.

You draw to yourself the persons who may be needed for the successful carrying out of your plans and purposes. In a similar manner, you are drawn toward those into whose plans and purposes you are suited to play an important part. In a nutshell, each person tends to attract toward himself whomever he needs in order to materialize his ideals and to express his desires.

These facts, as well as many others cited in this book, show that man can bring into materialization anything he can conceive mentally. Now I am prepared to show you a method that can increase the actual materialization power of your mind to bring you anything you desire through mind power alone! I call it . . .

THE HIDDEN BROTHERHOOD FOR TELECULT POWER

Nearly 2,000 years before Christ, it was said in the Upanishads, the sacred Vedic books of India, that if two people would unite their psychic forces, they could conquer the world, though singly they might be weak and uncertain of their power.

Then came Jesus, Who said, "Again I say unto you, that if two of you shall agree on earth as touching anything that they shall ask for, it shall be done for them of my Father which is in Heaven."

Why did Jesus send out His Disciples "two by two"? Why was it that on the one occasion when He visited His home town of Nazareth—*alone* among enemies—Jesus worked no mighty miracles? Why? Because, before a miracle could be wrought, there had to be faith—not only on Jesus' part, but on the part of one or more of those around Him. Read how often He told those He cured, "Thy faith hath made thee whole."

> **The simple fact is that if you add your prayers to mine, you get—not merely twice the power, but a hundred or a thousand times as much! Power that can literally move mountains!**

This is your Hidden Brotherhood for Telecult Power—any group of two or more persons that you can manage to get together to unite your psychic forces.

SECRET CEREMONIES OF THE HIDDEN BROTHERHOOD

Even if it's just you and one other friend, it's a Hidden Brotherhood. If you can manage to get together with this friend once a week, and actually agree on what you shall ask for and how you shall ask for it, you'll be amazed at the results!

Get together with each other, either in person, by letter or by phone. By phone, it's like an *Insta-Matic Dial-A-Wish Service* that actually works!

Confer with each other, talk over your difficulties and decide whose problem seems more pressing at the moment. Then agree on a specified time each day when—no matter where you are or what you're doing—you will each concentrate on the *same* prayer or request or command, to remedy this specific problem or difficulty.

Mind you, it is not enough to pray for the same thing. You must pray for the same thing *in the same way.* You may be praying for water, and I may be thinking about relieving my thirst. You may be praying for a car, and I may be thinking about my aching feet. You may be praying for money, and I may be thinking about the poverty and deprivation the lack of it is causing me. This is not the correct way to unite your psychic forces.

To make your Hidden Brotherhood work, all members must ask for the same thing, at the same time, in the same way. You may visualize this goal, as though you were looking at a picture of it, mentally. Or you may think about it in words. Or you may do both. With your friend, decide how beforehand. Furthermore, you must concentrate on the desired goal, not on the present circumstances.

Agree on a specific time each day (perhaps even two or three times a day) when—no matter where you are or what you're doing—you will each concentrate on the same prayer or request or command, to remedy the problem.

SPECIAL SECRETS OF THE HIDDEN BROTHERHOOD

If you decide to concentrate on a picture, you can use a picture of what you want, from a newspaper or magazine. It can be money, jewels, a new home or luxury such as a new car or a swimming pool. You will all need a copy of this same picture.

On the other hand, if you decide to use words, you must all use the exact same words. Once you have decided on the exact words (see the List that follows), and the time—or times—of day when you will both say them, you must realize that it is not necessary for you to say them aloud. You can memorize them, and repeat them to yourself at the appointed time—or you can read them silently from a piece of paper, on which you have written them.

In this manner, it is possible for you to broadcast silent messages to someone—in the presence of others—without uttering a single sound, to unite your psychic forces with this person, though the distance between you may be great, no matter where you happen to be, in an office or on a crowded bus or train.

But one thing of which you must make certain is that you will not be interrupted—that you will be able to concentrate—

at the appointed time. For nothing is more certain to break the invisible line of communication—and power—that exists between you and your Brothers (or Sisters) in spirit than an interruption.

If your group consists of two people, and you both can manage to be alone at the appointed times, a good way is to write your wish down on two pieces of paper, one for each of you. At the appointed time, each of you then concentrates on this paper—which is a kind of Cosmic Letter to the Master Mind of the Universe—with the Psychic Tele-Viewer described in Telecult Power #4.

In addition, even if a distance separates you, if you are in a place where no one will hear you, it is desirable to make your request aloud, in a chanting tone—for then these special words produce powerful thought currents that help you concentrate

LIST OF SECRET GROUP CHANTS

Here is a list of Secret Group Chants that you may say aloud, with your group, or read silently at the appointed times. You'll find one for any specific desire you may have. They are called Secret, because it must remain a secret known only to members of the group, that you are using this method. If it became known to outsiders, their skepticism might weaken your faith.

These Secret Group Chants are exactly like Hypnospells, re vealed in Telecult Power #3, without the special preparation, since—merely by uniting your psychic power with someone else's—you get thousands of times the power you get if you try it alone.

In the following examples, a dash indicates the name of the person for whom the request is being made. "Spell #" indicates its number in the continuing list of Hypnospells. In addition, some of these chants are labeled Photo-Form, for a reason that will be made obvious in the next chapter.

THE MAGIC MONEY CHANT
(Spell #11, also for use in games of chance)

Please bless ____ with new prosperity and a sudden increase in abundance. Starting now, and continuing for the rest of his days, let a golden river of glittering money pour into his life, filling it with sunshine, happiness and contentment. Let everything he touches turn to gold, and every enterprise or endeavor in which he is involved bring him the maximum rewards, without risk or loss of any kind. Shower him with his every want—for as long as he remains worthy. Let life make known unto him its joys, its happiness. Let life reveal to him the fruits of our faith, the ripe, rich, succulent fruits of good fortune. Let it proffer to him these offerings, for him to pluck to his heart's delight—to taste and savor endlessly for the rest of his days. For he is a good person, and will conduct himself in a manner worthy of the good fortune with which he is blessed—sharing and helping others along the way. Let him therefore know, now, any and all luxuries which he envisions for he is a true believer in the maxim, "If there is any good I can do my fellow man, let me do it now, for I shall pass this way but once."

—Photo-Form #1

THE MAGIC HEALTH CHANT (Spell #12)
FOR RELIEF OF PAIN

Let ____ regain his health. Let all his bodily functions become normal once again. Let that part of his body which is afflicted be bathed and soothed by the healing forces of nature. We are directing all our attention to . . . (mention the area), which will soon respond by feeling warm or tingly or both. We are directing all our thought, all our feeling, all our mental energy to this area and ____ will feel that increased energy.

With this increased energy will come more of everything the afflicted area needs. More blood rushes into and out of the area to carry off poisonous wastes. More antibodies come in with the blood to devour and carry off germs and viruses, and eliminate them in the natural way. More of the oxygen, iron, calcium, vitamins, minerals, enzymes and a host of other elements that living tissue needs is being brought in to nourish and revitalize this body.

All pain and discomfort will gradually fade away, as if by magic, and ____ will look better, feel better right now than he has in years, better in fact than most people do in their prime. Soon ____ will feel every muscle, gland and organ growing young and healthy again. And, what is more ____ will enjoy this new-found strength and youth to the fullest, regaining all the deep, strong confidence that only robust physical health can bring.

—Photo-Form #5

THE MAGIC CHANT TO MAKE YOU LOOK AND STAY YOUNG (Spell #13)

Let ____ become young again. Let ____ experience a remarkable rejuvenation. For age is but a state of mind, and not a matter of years. And ____ can be young if he (she) so chooses.

Mental energy directs physical energy. Let this new energy bestir youthful circulation to every inch of the body. Let this wonderful new supply of liquid refreshment surround each tiny cell with all the life-giving elements it needs—lymph, plasma and blood nutrients—to help ____ win back 10, 20, even up to 30 years of new youth, almost overnight!

We are going down deep within the body, speaking directly to the inner life centers, commanding them to grow young and strong again. For in many cases, those who have used this method claim that it has darkened silvery hair, helped relieve stomach trouble and wipe out painful backaches and stiff joints, that it has awakened new life in their glands and put a feeling of new youthfulness in their bodies.

Soon ____ will actually feel the years roll back as every tiny cell in his (her) body fills out, grows young and firm again. And when this happens, ____ will look fresher, younger, far more attractive!

—Photo-Form #6

THE MAGIC CHANT TO FIND A LOST OR MISPLACED ARTICLE (Spell #14)

Let this item (mention name of item) make its presence known to ____ as in a vision. Let the vibrations from this item (mention name of item) radiate strongly, impressing its image, and the image of its surroundings, upon the electron atmosphere around us. Let ____ receive these impressions on the screen of his mind, clearly and effortlessly, very soon now, when he least suspects it. Make his mental receiving equipment (the hidden antennae behind the eyes) as sensitive as a lightning rod to any impressions of a psychic nature. These impressions can be transmitted—and received—across a room, a city, or a continent, through solid walls, floors, ceilings and doors, for they are psychic energy, and psychic energy defies the laws of gravitational physics. By all the power behind the miracle of Life, we command this article to appear!

—Photo-Form #7

THE MAGIC CHANT OF POWER, SAFETY AND PROTECTION (Spell #15)

By these words, give ____ the mighty power to put down all foes, fend off all enemies. By these words, give ____'s words the power of a mighty iron fist. Give his arms, hands and legs the superhuman strength to serve him in times of crisis. Make his (her) body tough, strong and immune to all injury.

By these words, give ____ the mighty power to fend off all enemies with the aura of his body, which surrounds him like a psychic shield, and repells all evil influences.

By these words, which we now say, let this psychic shield appear and reappear—on command—whenever he (she) desires it. And let all evil influence bounce off this shield, like tiny beads off glass.

THE MAGIC CHANT TO WORK MIRACLES (Spell #16)

Let these words work their mighty miracles, just as they did for the sons of the children of Israel and the Disciples. If a miracle is needed, let that miracle happen. For the impossible is *possible* through psychic power. "What man *believes,* he can *receive,*" is a truth that can be taken literally. Let these words work a mighty miracle for ____, the miracle of (mention your desire) for they are true words, and true words are alive with power!

THE MAGIC CHANT FOR FINDING A PERFECT MATE (Spell #17) (bring your mate to you without asking)

Let ____ find his (her) perfect mate, soon. Let them be drawn to each other as the tide cleaves unto the shore. For this is a time for love. This is the time for desire. The single person who utters these words, alone or apart in spirit, desires a mate to satisfy the needs and fill the emptiness of his (her) life.

By these special words, let the perfect mate come rushing into ____'s life. Let this person possess all the qualities that ____ desires (mention what you want of him or her). And let ____ possess all the qualities that this person desires.

Let them be drawn to each other—though strangers they be now—by the invisible attractions of their strengths and weaknesses, and by the powerful desires which we express here now. Let each be the perfect mate in the other's eyes. And draw them to each other quickly.

—Photo-Form #8

THE MAGIC CHANT TO MAKE A CHILD OR SPOUSE OBEDIENT (Spell #18)

Make these children (or child) suddenly realize that they have but one mother (father, uncle, or aunt) and that they will be sorry if they do not take the feelings of this person—who has always loved them—into consideration, *and obey* for the sake of obeying, and because it is right to obey your elders.

Fill these children (or child) who are mindless even of their own good, who know not, and know not they know not, fill them with concern about the direction they are taking and what mistakes they are making, and what pitfalls they may avoid by heeding the advice of their parents.

Bring to them a sudden realization of what their lives would have been without their parents, and that even now they must not, they cannot take their parents for granted. Make them heed and obey.

* * *

For Husband or Wife, Use the Following Wording:

Make ____'s husband (wife) suddenly realize that he (she) has but one wife (husband), and that he (she) will be sorry if they do not take the feelings of this person —who has always loved them—into consideration, for the sake of love, and because it is right.

Fill (the person's name) with concern about the direction he (she) is taking and what mistakes he (she) is making, and what pitfalls he (she) may avoid by heeding the wife (husband).

Bring him (her) to a sudden realization of what his (her) life would have been without this person, and that even now they must not, they cannot take this person for granted. Make him (her) heed (or obey).

THE MAGIC CHANT TO RELIEVE INSOMNIA
(Spell #19) (Use in evenings only)

You are beginning to relax. Your legs are relaxed. . . . Your arms are relaxed. . . . Your entire body is relaxed. . . . Now you are enjoying complete relaxation. . . . Your legs are growing heavy . . . very heavy. . . . Your body is growing heavy . . . very heavy . . . your arms are growing heavy . . . very heavy . . . very heavy . . . your entire body is growing heavy . . . heavy . . . heavier . . . you feel as though you were deep, deep asleep . . . deeper and deeper . . . deeper and more relaxed . . . relaxing by stages . . . relaxing your entire body . . . arms relaxing . . . relaxing and heavy . . . heavy like lead . . . heavier and heavier . . . limp, heavy arms . . . heavier and heavier . . . every muscle, bone and tendon in your arm is relaxed and heavy . . . your hands are like lead . . . heavier and heavier . . . heavy like two lumps of lead . . . your left hand is heavy . . . heavier and heavier . . . the feeling is leaving your fingers, wrists and arms . . . heavy and relaxed . . . heavier and deeper . . . deeper and more relaxed . . . now your right hand . . . heavy and limp . . . limp and relaxed . . . limp and heavy . . . heavier and heavier . . . your right hand is almost numb . . . numb and heavy . . . heavier and heavier . . . both arms like lead . . . heavy like lead . . . heavy and deeper . . . deeper and more relaxed . . . deeper and heavier . . . heavier and heavier . . . your shoulders and your neck . . . relaxed and limp . . . relax your shoulders . . . let your shoulders relax . . . relaxed and comfortable . . . relax your neck . . . relaxed and comfortable . . . heavier and deeper . . . deeper and more relaxed . . . do not mind your body . . . your body feels heavy . . . heavy like a lump of lead . . . all the weight of your body is settling down . . . down . . . heavy like a lump of lead . . . heavier and heavier . . . relaxed and comfortable . . . your legs are growing heavy . . . heavier and heavier . . . all the weight of your body is settling down . . . down your legs . . . heavier and heavier . . . heavier and more relaxed . . . relaxed and losing all feeling . . . feeling heavy and relaxed . . . every muscle, bone and tendon in your legs is relaxed and heavy . . . your legs feel limp and heavy . . . heavier and heavier . . . heavy like a lump of lead . . . your left leg is heavy . . . your left leg is heavy and relaxed . . . your left leg is so heavy and relaxed that the feeling is draining out of it . . . leaving it relaxed and heavy . . . your left foot is so heavy and relaxed that it is plastered to the floor like a lump of clay . . . flat on the floor . . . flat on the floor . . . heavy and relaxed . . . your right foot is heavy . . . heavy like a lump of clay . . . heavy and relaxed . . . plastered to the floor . . . you cannot move your legs . . . you do not want to move your legs . . . relaxed and heavy . . . heavier and heavier . . . deep, deep . . . relaxing all over . . . relaxing completely . . . heavier and heavier . . . heavier and heavier . . . very heavy . . . very heavy . . . heavier and heavier . . . deep, deep . . . deep asleep . . . deep, deep asleep . . . now you are so deeply relaxed that you cannot open your eyes . . . you do not want to open your eyes because they feel heavy . . . very heavy . . . heavier and heavier . . . thousand-pound weights on your eyelids . . . dry and heavy . . . heavy and tired . . . tired and deep . . . deep, deep . . . deep asleep . . . try to open your eyes but you cannot. Sleep.

HOW EACH MEMBER OF YOUR TELECULT GROUP CAN GET ANYTHING HE WANTS!

Here is a typical example of how one such group got together to solve all sorts of difficulties for each other. They met at the house of one member of the group, and decided that each week the whole group would unite their thoughts—at a specified time each day—for one member of the group.

The first one chosen was Abe W., the owner of a small hardware store. He owed a great deal of money, and had no means of paying his debts. So that evening it was agreed that at noontime every day until the next meeting, each member would stop whatever he or she was doing, and spend a minute or two re peating the *Magic Money Chant*, silently or aloud, so that this man might receive the money he needed.

That week, for the first time in years, things really started happening for the store owner. A larger company, that operated a chain of such stores, and which was interested in developing new retail outlets in as yet undeveloped areas, approached him with a deal. In a letter which he received, they offered to renovate, enlarge, and completely restock his store—and retain him as manager and part-owner—if he would sell them an interest in his lease. This he agreed to, for a cash settlement of $20,000 plus a percentage of the weekly sales, which would amount to a very comfortable income. In addition, his son received news later that week, that he had been awarded a tuition-free scholarship to the school of his choice. And as if that were not enough, the largest of his creditors suddenly informed him that, due to an accounting error, he had been billed for a sizable amount more than a particular line of merchandise was worth—and that he was actually due for a refund, going back 5 years, and amounting to several thousand dollars.

The little store owner hurried to the next meeting of his Telecult Group, and excitedly informed them of what was happening. All the members were so elated over their success in helping the store owner that they chose the most difficult case of all as the next.

It was the wife of one of the members, Mrs. Julia K., who had lain immobile, in a spinal cast, for fifteen years. Sitting in silence, all the members of the group mentally pictured Mrs. K. strong and well, going about her work in a happy way. Then it was agreed that promptly at 12 noon each day until the next meeting, every member of the group would stop whatever he or she was doing and spend five minutes, silently willing that the woman would be free from pain, with the *Magic Chant for Health and Relief of Pain.*

All this, of course, was unknown to Mrs. K., who—on the second day of distance "treatment" by the Hidden Brotherhood —said that she thought, perhaps, she could sleep without sedation that night. On the third day, she asked if she could have the body cast removed. And on the fourth day, miraculously, she was able to sit up. On the sixth day, Mrs. K. was able to stand up for the first time since her illness. On the seventh day —her whole body quite flexible, and full of energy—she was able to walk about, completely unassisted.

A widow, Mrs. B., whose home was to be sold soon for failure to meet payments, was next. True to the law, just a day before the week was up, a well-to-do lady in town called and asked Mrs. B. if she would take care of her invalid aunt. The sum she offered would take care of the back payments on the home and give the widow a steady, lucrative income.

Mrs. D., the fourth member of the group, was having a quarrel with her husband. She was, in fact, living with her parents to avoid the difficulties she was encountering at home. Two days after the group began silently uniting their thoughts with the *Magic Chant to Make a Child or Spouse Obedient,* she began receiving letters from her husband, filled with the spirit of love, begging her to return.

The fifth member of the group was Richard G., a door-to-door toy salesman. It may have been lack of confidence, or even a bad line of toys, but Richard G. complained that he was just wearing out shoe leather, and having more doors slammed in his face than ever before. He turned his problem over to the Group.

Within days after the group began applying the *Magic Money Chant,* Richard G. began to hit a lucky winning streak that netted him 40 orders. Inside of one week, he sold 200 items.

Within a month, he sold 14,000 toys, many of them to toy stores. Two months later, he had a couple of salesmen working for him! Within a year, Richard G. was driving around in an air-conditioned Cadillac, and living in a $59,000 house, complete with swimming pool and all the modern conveniences. He had a business that practically ran itself.

> **Each and every member of that group got whatever he or she wanted!**

* * *

Recently, at the Psychodrama Institute, in California, it was reported that a group of ten people got together to see what problems they could solve for individual members of the group.

According to the Institute, this dramatic new method of helping people, long distance, really produces the desired results. During a two-year period, these group sessions have been nearly 100% successful. They have brought estranged family members together, performed seeming miracles in helping the sick, and even assisted in making financial gains possible. Somehow, the message that the group sends out always manages to help the intended subject.

INSTANTLY YOUR LIFE IS CHANGED

Do not wait for tomorrow, next week, or next month to use this method. There isn't any reason in the world why you shouldn't enjoy the riches, the happiness, the radiant health and peace of mind God meant for you to enjoy. And you can begin enjoying them today with Telecult Power.

The result may come instantly, or after a few days or weeks of accumulated effect. But results will definitely come—this I promise you—in the direction of your desired goal.

SUMMARY OF TELECULT POWER #6

1. In its ability to make things happen, your mind is like a Psychic Generator or Duplicating Machine that turns dreams into solid reality.
2. Radionic cameras have been devised which can photograph even a materializing thought.
3. There is a law of Mental Attraction that acts along lines very similar to the action of a giant magnet. That law may be stated as follows: each person tends to attract toward himself whomever or whatever he needs in order to materialize his ideals and to express his desires.
4. Man can bring into materialization anything he can conceive mentally.
5. A powerful way to increase the actual materialization power of your mind is to unite your prayers with someone else's. This gives you not merely twice the power, but thousands of times as much. Power that can literally move mountains!
6. Any group of two or more persons who unite for this purpose is called a Hidden Brotherhood.
7. To make your Hidden Brotherhood work, all members must ask for the same thing, at the same time, in the same way.
8. You can unite your psychic forces with another person no matter how great the distance between you, across a room, a city, or a continent, through solid walls, floors, ceilings or doors.
9. Once you have decided on the exact words you are going to use, you must realize that it is not necessary for you to say them aloud. You can repeat them to yourself at the appointed time—or you can read them silently from a piece of paper, on which you have written them.
10. One thing of which you must make certain is that you will not be interrupted at the appointed time. For nothing is

more certain to break the power that exists between you and your Brothers (or Sisters) than an interruption.

11. If you can manage to be alone at the appointed time, a good way is to concentrate on your wish with the Psychic Tele-Viewer described in Telecult Power #4.
12. If you are in a place where no one will hear you, it is desirable to make your request aloud in a chanting tone—for then these special words produce powerful thought currents that help you concentrate.
13. This chapter contains a list of Secret Group Chants that you may say aloud, with your group, or read silently at the appointed times. You'll find one for any specific desire you may have.
14. They are called secret because your using this method must remain a secret known only to members of the group.

TELECULT POWER #7

THE TELE-PHOTO TRANSMITTER:

How to Use Photo-Forms to Turn Your Dreams into Solid Reality

It has happened! Science has finally *proven* the existence of another world! An invisible world which seems to be the framework around which our own world is built!

I want to tell you all about it, because, right now, everything you need is in this invisible world—money, jewels, servants, fine possessions—everything, waiting for you to call upon it, waiting for you to teleport it into existence in this world, to materialize into solid reality that you can see and touch.

All you need to do this is an amazing psychic tool—already revealed to you earlier in this book—the amazing Hypno-Phone, which now becomes a Tele-Photo Transmitter. With it, you can teleport the object of your desire to you, from the invisible world!

This object—or person—whatever you desire, is in its transparent state, called a Photo-Form. The Tele-Photo Transmitter brings this object into focus, and photographs it psychically.

Once this happens, it slowly materializes and becomes visible for you to see, feel, touch and possess.

But before I tell you how to use your Tele-Photo Transmitter for this purpose, perhaps you are wondering: "What proof is there that an invisible world exists?" There is very definite proof —not only of an invisible world inhabited by objects and living beings—but that the mental energy which exists within us and directs and animates our bodies *survives!* And that the mind of man continues to think, plan and function. I call this new science of contact with the invisible world Spiritography.

SPIRITS SPEAK FOR THE RECORD

It has been reported that Friedrich Jergenson, a Russian-born Swedish artist, has made 80 tape recordings of voices purporting to be those of the spirit world.* One of Sweden's foremost sound experts, Kjell Stensson, of the State Radio, says the vioces could not be faked.

One of the recordings which Stensson says it would be impossible to fake is of voices interrupting a BBC broadcast of music to say, "We are not dead. We live. The contact. The contact." A total of 139 voices have been identified, some belonging to friends or historical figures.

THE VOICE WITHOUT A BODY

Among the most outstanding evidence we have of survival is the "Margery Mediumship." It began when Margery Crandon, a skeptical young woman, was suddenly able to receive messages from her brother, Walter.

The unusual part of it was that Walter's voice came from nowhere! It could speak from any part of a room. It was clear,

* Reported in *Fate* Magazine, Highland Park, Ill., December 1963. Reprinted by permission.

sharp and distinct. Nor was it in any way dependent upon a human voice.

Psychical research societies in many countries seized upon this opportunity to pursue their studies, and Margery Crandon's home was visited by hundreds of psychologists, scientists, and scholars from more than thirty countries, under conditions that made trickery impossible.

Once, one member of a group asked Walter to explain his voice. "How can I talk to you?" he laughed. "Simple. I take ectoplasm from Margery while she is in trance. I make a voice box out of it and use it to create sound vibrations." * (Ectoplasm is a filmy, plastic material which emerges at times from the mouth, nose, ears, or other orifices of a medium in trance and is able to take form and to exert physical pressure. It has been photographed many times as a solid substance, and at other times as a vapor.)

WHAT CONVINCED THE SCIENTISTS

In the Margery mediumship, Walter used an ectoplasmic hand for many of his demonstrations. With this hand he could make a pair of scalepans move up and down, carry objects—such as a coin—through thin air, and even make fingerprints. Extended investigations by the research officer of the American Society for Psychical Research established evidence that these prints were identical with the lifetime right thumbprint of Walter Stinson. A few of the prints could not be identified, and Walter said they were impressions from colleague spirits who aided him in the experiments. This phenomenon was actually photographed at one session. Two flash pictures were taken in a dimly lit room. In one, the film exposed through an ordinary glass lens showed only what the naked eye could see at the time—nothing. The other picture, taken with a quartz lens, revealed a tiny hand resting on the lower of two scalepans.

* From *A Life After Death* by S. R. Harlow and Evan Hill. © 1961 by S. R. Harlow and Evan Hill. Reprinted by permission of Doubleday & Company, Inc

The time required by Walter to build up psychic power (it took several sittings, each with little results, each taking about 45 minutes), his need of the traditional mediumship setup (a circle of people, in the dark, touching hands),* all seem to bear out the theory that an *electrical* intelligence survives the body—one which needs only *additional* electrical power to communicate with us. The members of a séance, sitting in a circle touching hands, form a good electrical circuit.

Since psychic power is electrical—at least *human* psychic power—it makes sense that a séance should be held in the dark. If you'll recall Telecult Powers #1 and #3, it was suggested that you practice receiving and sending in the early morning or late at night when the atmosphere is relatively free of interference, such as sunspot ions.

On a rare occasion when Walter did agree to carry messages from a departed friend to a member of the séance group (he disliked being what he called a "messenger boy"), he said: "Bates can't talk to you himself. He doesn't have the power to communicate." Then there was a faint whisper: "Hello, Ralph."

"Well," Walter said, "he does have some juice." There was silence, and Walter said, "But I guess it's all gone. I'll relay for you." †

All of this seems to lend credence to an opinion expressed many years ago by Dr. Cesare Lombroso, the physiologist and criminologist, who said: "There is a great probability now given us through psychical and spiritualistic researches that there is a continued existence of the soul after death, preserving a weak identity, to which the persistent soul can add new life and growth from the surrounding media." ‡

---

* The procedure is for a group to sit around a table of any size or shape. Each person then rubs his hands vigorously a few times, then places them flat on the table. Each person's thumbs should be crossed, and the little finger of each hand outstretched, touching the little finger of the next person's hand. (This is also the procedure for table tipping. A spirit is then asked to tip the table if he is present—once for yes, twice for no. Questions are then asked, with this yes-or-no code.)

† S. Ralph Harlow and Evan Hill, *A Life After Death.*

‡ James Hyslop, *Enigmas of Psychical Research* (Boston, Mass.: Herbert B. Turner Co., 1906).

"Weak" only to us, however, because from all the evidence we have, departed spirits seem to be able to see each other quite clearly. For example, on the occasion just mentioned, when a member of the séance asked Walter to contact a friend, Walter soon replied that he saw the place where the friend now resided, and then described this person.

ASTRAL PROJECTION

There is one persistent claim, among the *living*, that would seem to substantiate an afterlife. And that is the phenomenon of astral projection. The thought of a person leaving his body and wandering about as an amorphous mass of mobile intelligence is a startling concept. Yet despite accusations of everything from fraud to out-and-out insanity, those who insist that they have experienced astral projection steadfastly maintain that they are telling the absolute truth. Among these people are several eminent scientists!

LISTENS TO THE "HEARTBEAT" OF A SPIRIT

Dr. Hans Gerloff, in his book *Die Phantome von Kopenhagen*, shows many photographs of apparently otherwise invisible beings, taken by Gerloff himself with infrared rays. He also claims that he has listened to what seemed to be the heartbeats of several "materializations" through a stethoscope, has had these beings breathe through a tube into a bottle of limewater (which turns white when air is introduced), and, in one instance, was kissed on the forehead by a departed friend.

It is difficult to doubt the sincerity of Dr. Gerloff, and of the many distinguished scientists who assisted him in his investigations. As a possible explanation, he offers the theory of "ideoplasty," or thought-forms, which is the subject of this chapter.

NEW EVIDENCE OF LIFE IN AN INVISIBLE WORLD

At the Delwarr Laboratories, Oxford, England, radionic instruments have been devised which, by tuning in on radiations, can photograph the *future, matured form of a flower from its ungerminated seed!*

These and many other new discoveries seem to have brought to light a new world! An invisible world which seems to be the framework around which our own world is built! A world that may very well be inhabited by unseen dwellers; a world in which invisible animals exist, perhaps, that can guard your house, protect your family, carry messages; a world in which poltergeists exist that can make furniture move, cups and saucers fly about, stones to fall from mid-air; as well as elementals and "little people"—tiny beings that have been called by many names over the centuries, elves, gnomes, fairies, leprechauns.

Do they really exist? Nandor Fodor tells us of photos taken of them in modern times. They may lead you to a buried "pot of gold," although it may be different from what you expect, grant your wishes, and much more.*

If visual images can survive as vibrations in the electron atmosphere around us, if sound can do the same (as in the case of echoes), if, indeed, each and every one of us is part of a Super-intelligence that created all matter, is it not reasonable that we ourselves survive in some form, as intelligent beings?

Is it not possible, for example, that the electrical circuitry of the brain could survive independently of its physical housing in the same manner that sights and sound survive?

In experiments such as those with Ted Serios, for example, it has been shown that photographs of buildings which have long since been torn down can still be taken. Why? Because all mat-

* And if evil spirits do exist, then the Psychic Shield of Telecult Power #3 may also be described as a spiritual lightning rod that wards off psychic attack.

ter consists of atoms which are always in motion, constantly circling each other. In electricity, every initial impulse sets up a wave vibration in the electron sea which lasts forever. Why not the brain—and even the body?

An interesting, though unscientific, bit of evidence in support of the theory that some form of electrical intelligence survives the body is an item that appeared in the May 1966 issue of *Fate* Magazine by Phyllis R. Haag, whose brother appeared to her in a dream to bring her news of something that was happening hundreds of miles away.

"As my brother turned to go I asked how he could visit me when he was dead," she reports. "He reached out and touched my hand, imploring me not to be afraid. As our hands touched . . . an electrifying shock raced up my arm, instantly awakening me . . . with such a start that at first I thought my hand had come in contact with a live electrical circuit." *

HOW TO USE PHOTO-FORMS TO TURN YOUR DREAMS INTO REALITY!

Your Hypno-Phone or Tele-Photo Transmitter, becomes a kind of magic or psychic camera when used to teleport the object of your desire to you, from the invisible world. When you dial the Photo-Form you desire, this camera photographs its invisible, protoplasmic form, which then slowly becomes visible!

You may recall that Telecult Power #6 gave several group chants or hypnospells. All of these are really Photo-Forms. A Photo-Form is a word picture or word description that refers to a definite person or object, a form. To put it another way, a Photo-Form is a desire, expressed in special words which produce powerful thought currents.

The Tele-Photo Transmitter is a kind of powerful psychic

* Reprinted by permission of *Fate* Magazine, Highland Park, Ill.

camera, whose photo-glass—like a magnifying glass—sends your thoughts like a burning streak of lightning to their destination in the invisible world.

When you concentrate on any of the Photo-Forms on the next few pages with your Tele-Photo Transmitter, you bring your desire into sharp, clear focus. You *photograph* it psychically, at which point it *must* materialize. (For this is the actual Law of Creation of the Universal Mind.)

Figure H. Hypno-Phone becomes a Tele-Photo Transmitter.

TELEPORTS OBJECT 300 MILES WITH A PHOTO-FORM

As an example of how a Photo-Form or Tele-Command works, Catherine Ponder in her book *The Dynamic Laws of Healing,** reports how one of her students who had lost a small golden jewelry box, used such a group of words to recover a lost object. This woman had left the box while visiting at the home of some friends, 300 miles away. When she came home and discovered

* Catherine Ponder, *The Dynamic Laws of Healing* (West Nyack, New York: Parker Publishing Co., Inc., 1964).

the loss, she was overwhelmed with grief. She sat before an empty dressing table, and spoke these words:

"Lord, a dear and treasured object has been taken from me —one that cannot be replaced and means a great deal to me. I *know* that you will help me in this matter because you are kind and just. And so, in advance, I am thanking you for this help."

Then she turned from the empty table and rose to finish unpacking. For several minutes she was completely absorbed in this work. Suddenly she inadvertently turned toward the table —and, lo and behold, there sat the jewelry box! A true case of teleportation!

LIST OF PHOTO-FORMS

Here is a list of Photo-Forms you can dial with your Tele-Photo Transmitter, as revealed in Telecult Power #6, "Special Secrets of the Hidden Brotherhood"—the difference being that if you decide to use your Tele-Viewer, you do not need another person to concentrate and join his psychic forces with yours:

Photo-Form #1—Money (revealed in Telecult Power #6)

Photo-Form #2—Jewels

Bring me jewels beyond description. Bring me rich, glittering diamonds, emeralds, rubies and pearls. Coming into view, speeding toward me from the invisible world. This Psychic Tele-Viewer will bring me all these things and more—shiny rings, bracelets, pin-holders, cuff-links, and baubles, made of thick, genuine gold, platinum, silver and other precious metals. In the name of the Law of Creation, I direct the invisible forces to bring these things to me, for in the beginning there was the Word!

Photo-Form #3—A New Home

Bring me a lovely new home, in a beautiful country or suburban setting, that I will be proud to own. Make this home the pride of myself, my family, my loved ones. Give it large, lovely, clean, comfortable rooms, with beautiful picture windows, ample closet space, and all the latest conveniences. Make this structure sturdy and well-built, complete with finished basement and a two-car garage. Give it a new, modern kitchen with all automatic appliances. Give it the exact number of bedrooms I need, completely furnished, each with its own bath facilities. Give it a living area and recreation room, complete with a library, billiard table, large-screen color television set, comfortable carpeting and easy chairs. Make this home cool in the summer and warm in winter, with its own outdoor recreational facilities—a garden, a patio (complete with tables and chairs), and a swimming pool. Make it the perfect home in every way.

Photo-Form #4—A New Automobile

Bring me a new automobile, all shiny and clean. Give it a well-built, precision-crafted motor that will run endlessly, free of repairs. Equip this car with power brakes, power steering, power windows, automatic speed control, and all safety devices. Give it beautiful new upholstery and carpeting, plus its own radio-telephone equipment. Give it brand-new tires of the thickest, safest type, and make it ride as smooth as velvet.

Photo-Form #5—To Heal and Relieve Pain (see in previous chapter, "The Magic Health Chant for Relief of Pain.")

Photo-Form #6—To Look and Stay Young (see in previous chapter, "The Magic Chant to Make You Look and Stay Young.")

Photo-Form #7—To Find A Lost Article (see in previous chapter, "The Magic Chant to Find A Lost or Misplaced Article.")

Photo-Form #8—To Find the Perfect Mate (see in previous chapter, "The Magic Chant for Finding a Perfect Mate.")

AMAZING USE OF PHOTO-FORM #1—MONEY

Lillian P., a widow, says she felt silly using it but thought it was worth a try, since she had a family to support. She happened to be holding her checkbook in her hand—she was always paying bills—when she dialed Photo-Form #1, with her Tele-Photo Transmitter.

When she looked around and saw nothing, she thought, "Well, it serves me right." A short time later, however, when her monthly bank statement arrived, she happened to notice a balance $100 higher than her checkbook showed.

Was it luck or coincidence? Apparently, in the normal routine of checking, the bank had corrected a simple arithmetical error that she had made.

• • •

In an amazing case history revealed in Chapter 9, you'll see how a little girl, who probably used the Photo-Form for Money without realizing it, received a shower of money—which came, seemingly, out of thin air!

PHOTO-FORM BRINGS DIAMONDS

A woman of my acquaintance, a very good friend whose opinions I respect, stubbornly insisted that the whole science of Photo-Forms was a lot of nonsense. I pointed out to her that scientists have actually succeeded in crystallizing diamonds out of thin air.

I said, "Is it no more reasonable that Photo-Forms should work than that heavy machines can fly as well as can birds, or that a picture can travel across the ocean and wind up in a TV tube?"

She jokingly replied that if a Photo-Form could work, it ought to be able to bring her jewels beyond description. I accepted her challenge and told her to dial Photo-Form #2, with a Tele-Photo Transmitter.

This she did, while I watched. Then she looked up at me, smiling, as if to say, "I told you so. Look, there's nothing on the desk." Then she heard a tiny tinkle, like metal hitting the floor. She looked under the desk, and there was a nickle, a dime and a quarter. Her jaw dropped open, and then she laughed. "It's just some change. It must've dropped accidentally." The spell was operating.

That morning, on the way to lunch, she found two tiny gold earrings on the staircase. I was there, and saw it. The next day, at the office, I saw her wearing a pearl necklace, and a pair of thin silver bracelets. She covered her mouth and giggled, saying her husband had surprised her with these presents the night before.

A few days later, she came to my office, and sat down. "I got some presents in the mail," she said. "A set of gold cuff-links, and a beautiful gold pin-holder, from my daughter. I found this on the front lawn this morning," she said. It was a platinum ring set with emeralds and diamonds. "I don't know who it belongs to. I'll ask around and put an ad in the papers." Several answers came, but no one gave the right description. So it was hers to keep!

HOW YOUR SERVANTS IN THE INVISIBLE WORLD RESPOND TO TELE-COMMANDS

As was mentioned before, there are roughly two types of beings in the invisible world: departed spirits, and servants.

These servants or little people ("little men" as they have sometimes been called) can be quite useful to you if you know how to use them. For they are neophyte spirits, still earning the right to become human, and they must obey.

They respond, however, only to certain words known as Tele-Commands. A Tele-Command is anything from a specific request, such as the Hypnospells, Group Chants, and Photo-Forms, to single words or Solo-Words. To increase the power of your contact with the invisible world, you may continue to use your Psychic Tele-Viewer, which now becomes a Tele-Communicator, over which you can broadcast these commands.

An example of a Tele-Command is the following incantation, used by certain country folk in the heart of South Carolina to bring about a healing:

Angels three that never fail,
Michael, Gabriel, Azreal,
Azreal dark, Gabriel light,
Michael altogether bright!
Thou, (the name of the person)
Born the (day, month, and year)
. . . When I passed by thee
And saw thee suffering, I said, "Heal and Be Well";
Yes, I said unto thee, "Heal and Be Well."
Thus say I unto thee.
Haste, ye blessed angels three!
Haste, thou blessed trinity!

Bible students will recognize the main part of the incantation as coming from the 16th Chapter of Ezekiel. It is said that all the incantations of this sort, derive from Holy Scripture, or call upon the angels or God.

HOW THE "LITTLE PEOPLE" RESPOND TO SOLO-WORDS AND LUCKY NUMBERS

The "little people" of the invisible world also respond to single words of command, called Solo-Words. Here is the only complete listing of Solo-Words that I have been able to uncover, together with the Lucky Numbers that actually stand for Solo-Words, and are a kind of secret code of communication:

ro-ama (11) = new youth
breemar (16) = good health

lola (12) = love
shoras (2) = romance
trinka (5) = money
ouma (7) = new friends
hora (4) = wisdom
oom-rama (9) = power (control)
owaye (22) = protection
swa-soon (8) = relief from pain
on-ra (3) = win an argument
car-dual (15) = marital harmony
yano (101) = find (object)
poindu (14) = remember (something forgotten)
zenda (77) = remember (memorize)
or-con-dorr (63) = power to understand
lanid (19) = decode distorted messages
ordway (20) = transportation
tone-a-tone (43) = new pep and energy
alon-alon (28) = help
swa-swasoon (39) = relax
lin-rama (71) = win respect
owlet (92) = dissolve grudge
hinch (49) = make time stand still
tavano (31) = win at games of chance
aron-aron-los (41) = escape

Solo-Words are generally used for what one might call small miracles. Although powerful in spurts, and excellent in times of crises, when help is needed fast, they are generally less powerful than the longer Tele-Commands. Moreover, they are not English words, but have been derived from the accidental discoveries of those who speak in "Tongues."

USES TELE-COMMAND FOR A POCKETFUL OF MONEY

Jerry D. reports that he was broke, a week before payday, and couldn't go anywhere or do anything because he had no cash. All he did, he says, was to say the Tele-Command (or Photo-Form) for Money. He had no idea where the money would come from—or if it would come at all. It was Saturday morning, so he decided to have a cup of coffee, and go out and get a haircut (on credit). He went to the closet, put on a jacket, reached in the pocket—without thinking—and lo and behold! His hand closed around a small billfold with several dollars that he had apparently left in the jacket last Spring.

FILLS EMPTY PURSE

Mrs. Emma G. reports she needed a few extra dollars for shopping, so she used the Tele-Command (or Photo-Form) for Money. Suddenly she remembered her husband's habit of stashing small amounts of money away around the house—but where? She had hunted for it before without success. This time, however, a hunch led her straight to the edge of the living room carpet. She reached under the carpet and, to her surprise, found an envelope containing about $20 in cash!

USES TELE-COMMAND FOR ROMANCE

Anne G., 48, was—in her own words—"a lonely old spinster." To make matters worse, she was slightly overweight. But she was still "looking." Trouble was, the men she liked never seemed to like her. When she learned of this method of Tele-Commands, she decided to use it on one man, in particular, whom she had seen at church socials, but who never seemed to notice her. The very next time she caught his eye—to say hello—she used the Tele-Command for Love. He responded with a polite hello, started to turn away, then suddenly turned back and introduced himself to her, with a smile.

Just as they began talking, Anne noticed another gentleman she liked, who never seemed to notice her. And she used this Tele-Command again. Within a short space of time, a whole group of men were clustered about her, and she was the center of attention. She felt glamorous, attractive, and wanted—for the first time. In the days that followed, this and all the other

Tele-Commands never failed her—and she proceeded to make up for what she called her "lost youth."

TELE-COMMAND BRINGS MATE WITHOUT ASKING

Mrs. Conrad B. reports that she was tired of "pursuing" her husband, as she called it. She wanted him to voluntarily do the things she longed for—show affection, take her places, and enjoy life. But, she said, he hadn't looked at her in years! He would fall asleep immediately after supper, or watch the ball games, or read the papers. Sometimes, in fact, he would just disappear all day, without telling her where he was going! Finally one day at breakfast, Mrs. B. silently used the Tele-Command for Love and the Tele-Command to Win Respect.

Instantly, the expression on her husband's face changed, from boredom to interest. He began talking to her, and showing more interest than he had in years! He began making plans to take her places. And that evening he brought her a surprise gift. Together, now, they are enjoying life and their love is ten times stronger than it ever was!

HOW TO TALK TO BEINGS IN THE INVISIBLE WORLD!

In spirit contact, the Tele-Photo Transmitter or Hypno-Phone of Telecult Power #4 becomes a kind of telephone through which you may speak to the "little people" of the invisible world. To use it, the same rules apply that apply to Telecult Hearing, Telecult Vision and Thought Projection. Your Hypno-Phone actually aids the natural "sending" and "receiving" equipment that you were born with.

SPIRIT TELEPHONE HELPS FIND MONEY

Spirit beings face the same problems in trying to make themselves "heard" by the living that the living have in trying to receive thoughts from other living persons. The living mind is constantly having mental energy drawn off to regulate the body. Housed in its physical body, the mind is constantly besieged with earthly problems, which it must solve with earthly limitations. It is these factors which tend to block reception, but which may be overcome with the receiving techniques—especially Deep Relaxation—recommended for Telecult Hearing and Telecult Vision.

But spirits *can* contact you with the mental earphone that you possess. In fact, *all* the methods in this section and the next are really spirit telephone techniques, although various kinds of equipment are used to help in this process. When you use these various devices, you help increase the power of your mental mechanism; and these methods are bound to work for you because, in using them, you are doing your share to meet the spirit world more than half way.

The spirits, too, have their methods for increasing their power to communicate with the living, and they are often able to do so without help.

There are innumerable instances on record, for example, of "spirit voices" telling people where to look, or what to do to find money, as when a "spirit voice" tells someone to bet on a certain horse. Many of the examples given in Telecult Power #9 are clear examples of voices of spirits being received in a telephone like manner.

DID EDISON DISCOVER THE SPIRIT TELEPHONE?

All his life, Thomas Edison was an agnostic. He would neither believe nor disbelieve in survival. Privately, he was inclined to disbelieve. But this was an opinion he seldom expressed, and then only to close friends.

It was not until five years before his own death in 1931 that Edison began to meditate more seriously about survival and discuss it at great length in his writings and among his close associates. If the human personality survives death, he reasoned, there ought to be a way to contact spirits mechanically. A machine to talk to the dead. Or a mechanical device which spirits could use to contact the living. If this were possible, it would settle the question of survival once and for all.

Edison proceeded to tackle the problem with all the vigor and persistence that had characterized his earlier efforts. Rumors about his work began to crop up every now and then, but because Edison would not comment about his work, these rumors died down. Suddenly, after months of research, Edison began talking, among friends and in scientific circles, as though he definitely believed in survival, and as though life in an invisible world were a certainty.

What had happened to make Edison change his mind?

To this day, no one is sure. If Edison did invent a machine to talk with the dead, it was never found or made public. And Edison took the secret to the grave with him.

More than likely Edison *did* discover a machine to communicate with the invisible world—the same that modern science has finally discovered. I refer to your own psychic machinery, the psychic equipment we are all born with—the Mental Earphone, the Psychic Tele-Viewer, the Spirit Telephone or Tele-Communicator, and other powers.

SUMMARY OF TELECULT POWER #7

1. Science has finally proven the existence of an invisible world, which seems to be the framework around which our own world is built.
2. Right now, everything you need is in this invisible world—money, jewels, servants, fine possessions—everything, in its beginning or protoplasmic state, waiting to be materialized into solid reality.
3. There is definite proof of an invisible world, inhabited by

objects and lifelike beings—as well as proof that the mind of man survives.

4. All you need to materialize the object—or person—you desire from this invisible world is your Psychic Tele-Viewer.
5. Such an object—in its transparent state—is called a Photo-Form. Your Psychic Tele-Viewer brings it into focus, and photographs it psychically. Once this happens, it slowly materializes for you to see, feel, touch and possess.
6. You may dial any Photo-Form you desire, with your Psychic Tele-Viewer. The Photo-Forms in this chapter are really word-descriptions, or word pictures, of any desire you may have. When you concentrate on one with your Psychic Tele-Viewer, you photograph it psychically, at which point it must begin to materialize.
7. There are roughly two types of beings in the invisible world: departed spirits, and servants.
8. The servants or little people ("little men" as they have sometimes been called) can be quite useful to you if you know how to use them. For they are neophyte spirits, still earning the right to become human, and they must obey.
9. The "little people," or servants, of the invisible world respond only to certain words known as Tele-Commands, contained in this book.
10. To increase the power of your contact with the invisible world, you may use your Tele-Communicator, over which you can broadcast these commands.
11. The "little people" of the invisible world also respond to single words of command, called Solo-Words. This chapter contains a complete list of them.
12. Lucky Numbers actually stand for Solo-Words, and are a kind of secret code of communication with the invisible world. The Lucky Number for each word is given in this list.
13. You may use a kind of Spirit Telephone to contact the invisible world. This telephone consists of the same sending

and receiving equipment described in earlier chapters, such as the Mental Earphone (Telecult Power #1).

14. All the methods in this section and the next are really spirit telephone techniques, although various kinds of equipment are used to help in this process. When you use these various devices, you help increase the power of your mental mechanism.

TELECULT POWER #8

HOW TO MAKE AND USE "A MAGIC MONEY BAG" TO RECEIVE GIFTS FROM THE INVISIBLE WORLD

In contact with the invisible world, there is a device which I call a Spirit Finger or Compass. This consists of any object, including the human hand, which a spirit may use to point to something, and thereby convey a message.

In spiritual healing, for example, the spiritualist may point his hand up and down a sick person's body. By stopping his hand at the appropriate point, a spirit doctor can indicate to the spiritualist the location of the trouble.

A spiritualist may ask his spirit guides to indicate the location of some person, place or thing by running his finger over a map. A date may be ascertained by running your finger down a column of figures representing successive years, and again down a list of months, days, hours, etc. The Abbé Mermet was said to have obtained phenomenal results this way in finding out facts for people that could be ascertained in no other way.

A MAGIC WAND TO FIND YOU MONEY!

Spirit contact by means of an object that the spirit is asked to move is known as divination. One remarkable form of divination is known as "dowsing." It makes use of a kind of "magic" wand that acts as a directional compass.

The interesting fact is that anyone can try it for himself. Almost any wood will do for a dowsing rod. Hazel was chosen in 16th century Europe because of its availability and flexibility (the spirit who is guiding you will often bear down on the rod and make it bend).

Instead of a forked stick, you can use a wire coat hanger, by bending it in the center so that the hanger forms a Y. Bend the ends of the Y slightly outward, grip them in the usual fashion, and use the hook of the hanger as the pointer. Another excellent rod can be formed from two long corset stays. Simply tape them together for about a third of their length. Then bend the loose ends outward as the points of the Y.

MAGIC COMPASS DETECTS ENEMY TUNNELS

The New York Times of October 13, 1967 carried an article headed "Dowsers Detect Enemy's Tunnels." The article, written by Hanson W. Baldwin, was datelined Camp Pendleton, California and described how Marine Corps engineers both in their training and under actual battle conditions in Vietnam are using improvised divining rods (made out of wire coat hangers) to detect tunnels, mines and booby traps. Mr. Baldwin states that he tried it himself and located a tunnel, much to his surprise, In this case, the rod sloped downward, which—he was told—indicated that the tunnel had a downward slope. Major Nelson Hardacker of the Fifth Marine Division stated that the device worked for virtually all who used it.

HOW TO USE A "MAGIC MONEY BAG" TO RECEIVE GIFTS FROM THE INVISIBLE WORLD

Another device used for spirit contact, one which the spirit is asked to move, is a kind of "Magic Bag" known as an exploratory pendulum. It is easy to set up a code of communication with any spirit by means of this device.

The exploratory pendulum can be traced back to ancient Greece and a form of divination called coscinomancy. Two people would hold a sieve or strainer suspended by strings and put questions to it. As the strainer moved, a design would be traced on the ground by the sand running through it. The design would then be interpreted by an oracle.

From this crude pendulum, more refined forms evolved, such as that of a small crystal ball suspended from a chain, or a pear-shaped pendulum carved from ebony or ivory. Plastic pendulums have recently come into vogue, and these, like some of their predecessors, are hollow, so that they can be filled with a sample of the substance sought. In place of this you may use a small leather bag, plastic cup, rag, or handkerchief—containing the desired substance—suspended from a string.

The exploratory pendulum helps explain how a spirit could possibly know the location of water, or gold, or some other object. And that is through the power of *radiesthesia* which both living and spirit beings possess. Radiesthesia is simply the ability of the mind to pick up the vibrations that all objects (and gases) give off (see "A Homemade Antenna That Picks Up Thoughts," page 40; also "How Visual Impressions Are Received Astrally," page 54). Spirits, since they are entirely psychic beings, unshackled by the demands of the physical body, are naturally more sensitive to such vibrations. Nevertheless you possess the same ability, and you may prove it to yourself in the following manner.

Take any straight object, such as a ruler or a pencil, and

place it at any angle on a table. Construct a pendulum, consisting of a ring or key suspended by a string about twelve inches long. Hold the string between your thumb and forefingers, allowing your hand to hang limply from the wrist. Rest your elbow on the table, so that the object dangles freely over the center of the ruler.

The pendulum will begin to move back and forth with a straight swing, *but along the line of the ruler.* The hand may be shifted to different places along the ruler, but with the same result, the interesting point being that this is not the usual circular motion. The direction is governed by the ruler, as though it exerted a magnetic power. If the pendulum is brought to one end of the ruler, the swinging will stop and the pendulum will begin to rotate.

Thus, in exploring for water, you would fill the pendulum with water, or in some way manage to suspend a small container of water from a string. You would hold this pendulum suspended—and quite still—over patches of land you wished to explore. If the pendulum began to swing, especially in a swirling fashion, it would indicate the presence of water.

If divining for gold, you would use gold. You would proceed in a similar manner for silver, diamonds, platinum, or even deposits of coal or oil.

Many gas and pipeline companies and municipal water companies use dowsing in their everyday work. One of today's leading oil companies used a barefoot Indian who located oil wells for them through a certain "feeling" he got in his feet.

For spirit contact, the pendulum is used to set up an actual code of communication. To do so, proceed as before. Rest your elbow on a desk or table or any flat surface so that the pendulum dangles freely.

Now there are only four directions in which this pendulum can move (see Figure I). By moving the pendulum, a spirit will show you which direction means "*Yes,*" which means "*No,*" which means "*I don't know,*" and which means "*I don't want to answer that question.*"

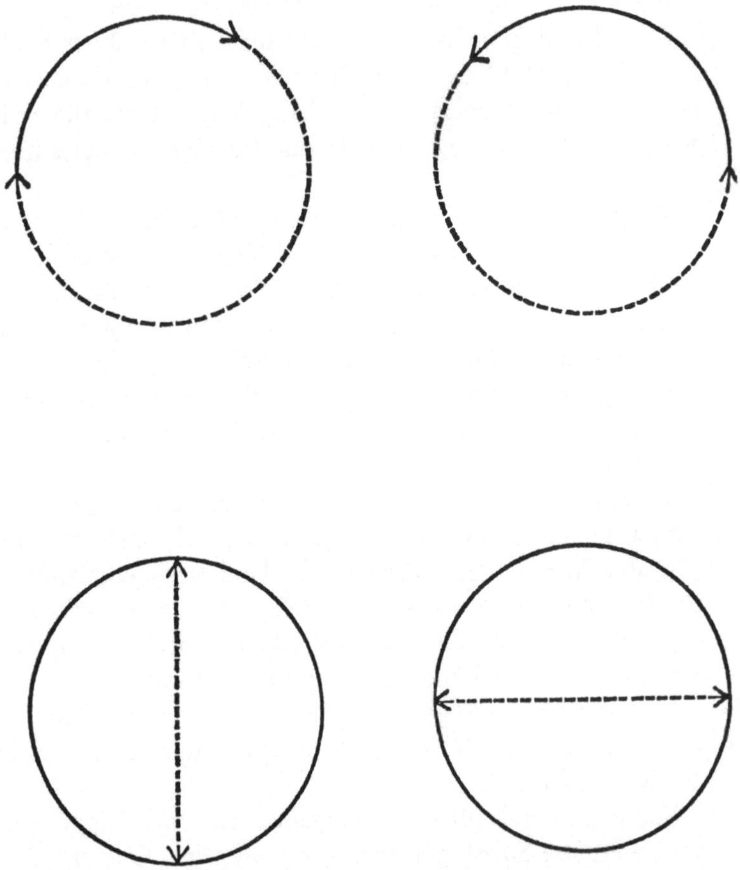

Figure I.

Hold the pendulum perfectly still, and say: "Will a member of the spirit world who can answer my questions concerning (and you name the general subject, such as money, love, etc.) please come forward." No words are needed. Just think the request. In a few moments, the pendulum should begin to swing of its own accord.

Now you proceed to establish a code: "Will this spirit please select a motion of the pendulum which is to mean 'Yes.'" The pendulum should move in one of the four directions. Follow the same procedure for "No," "I don't know," and "I don't want to answer that question." (For these last two, the motion of your pendulum may be the same, or it may remain still.)

At this point, you may ask your spirit guide any question you desire. But be sure that your question is so clear that it can be answered with a simple "Yes" or "No." Ask only one question at a time, and each time wait for your answer.

NOTE: sometimes two or three minutes will pass before the pendulum begins to move, though more often it does so very quickly. If it does not move, try clearing your mind of all thoughts except the question you are asking; or put the pendulum aside and try again later, when you are more relaxed. For some reason, tension always seems to hinder contact.

MAGIC COMPASS PREDICTS SEX OF UNBORN CHILD

Receiving guidance this new way, I'm sure, will be a fascinating matter for you. You may have a choice to make, or a problem that calls for knowledge that you do not possess. The inhabitants of the invisible world have access to all knowledge—past, present, and future.

Leslie LeCron in his book *How to Make the Next Ten Years the Best Years of Your Life,** reports a fascinating use of the pendulum technique:

> One day, a young woman patient complained to me that she was having much (difficulty) in the pelvic area. She said she had just seen her physician, a gynecologist. He had examined her, thinking it might be a tubal pregnancy, but could find no reason for the pain. She asked if pendulum answers could tell us anything about it, so some were asked. In reply to one question as to whether there

* Leslie LeCron, *How to Make the Next Ten Years the Best Years of Your Life* (West Nyack, N.Y.: Parker Publishing Co., Inc., 1966).

> was a tubal pregnancy, the answer was affirmative. Next day . . . she went back to her doctor, and with a more thorough examination he found that she did have a tubal pregnancy. The answer had been right.

Another fascinating feature of the pendulum is this: if held above a man's head, the pendulum will swing back and forth (usually in a sideways direction); when held above a woman's head, it will gyrate in a circle. With some operators, these actions are reversed, sometimes depending on whether the operator is right- or left-handed. However, it is usually so dependable with each individual operator that the pendulum has come to be known, among mind scientists, as the "sex detector."

An interesting bit of research has been carried out with several obstetricians and other doctors cooperating and reporting their results. Specifically, they wanted to know: Could the pendulum method reveal the sex of an unborn child of a pregnant woman? "Using this questioning method in 402 cases there were 360 correct predictions—90 percent," reports Dr. LeCron. "Most of the failures seemed to occur when the prediction was the same as the sex preferred by the mother. Wishful thinking may have influenced the answers then."

This method has also been used as a way of locating some lost object; of finding out if it was stolen or mislaid and forgotten. Still another way that this questioning can be used is in trying to find the interpretation and meaning of some dream.

Another fascinating use of the pendulum is the time-telling test. Here, the pendulum—preferably an ordinary finger ring—is dangled into a drinking glass. The operator then calls upon the pendulum, or its spirit guide, to tell the time in hours, and the device obligingly does so. It swings back and forth, increasing its speed until it begins to clink the sides of the glass—"one, two, three, four, five"—ending on the exact hour and slackening its swing immediately thereafter. Sometimes it will add a trifling "plunk" for a half-hour, often to the surprise of the operator himself.

When this time-telling test was in its heyday, a few generations ago, skeptics used to get up in the night and try out the pendulum for themselves, without looking at the clock. According to the majority of the reports, the dangling ring gave them the right time!

A PHOTO-READING CHARACTER ANALYZER AND DO-IT-YOURSELF LIE DETECTOR

Here is an experiment which will prove to you that there are more forces at work in this world than you suspect. Take a small compass and tie a string to it. Tie the other end of the string to the middle of a pencil, leaving about six inches of string between the two objects. Place a photograph of someone on the desk or table before you. Holding the pencil at both ends, suspend the compass above the photograph (prop your elbows on the table).

Now ask the compass questions about the person in the photograph. "Yes" will be signaled by the compass moving up and down over the photograph. "No" will cause the compass to move from side to side.

In this manner the pendulum—or spirit finger—becomes a kind of homemade lie detector that is surprisingly accurate. But first it is a good idea to test the invisible force which is moving the compass to determine whether it is a mischievous spirit, or one that can be trusted. If you ask a spirit if it will help you hurt somebody and it says yes, it is not to be trusted.

OW YOU CAN RECEIVE COSMIC LETTERS

Some of the most intriguing evidence we have of the survival of the human personality after death comes from automatic writing and automatic speech. An automatist is not a medium in the usual sense and does not go into trance, although some slight dissociation—that is, lack of awareness of one's surroundings—does take place in most cases. "Automatic" phenomena are of two types, written and spoken. In the former, the automatist simply sits down and writes whatever comes to mind, and in the latter, speaks it with someone else taking it down. The association-of-ideas test in psychology, where the subject writes a word, such as "father," and then follows it with a series of words suggested by the word, is really automatism.

* * *

Research in automatic writing seems to indicate that many spirit messages bypass the conscious mind (as in peripheral vision) and are received directly by the sensitive cortex. Such a message may only be released automatically—as in dreams, sudden hunches, or inexplicable memories or flashes of insight, triggered by a thought or situation similar to the forgotten memory. *Or* it can be discovered among many subconscious thoughts through automatic speech or writing.

When you hold a soft pencil or a ball-point pen in your hand, your inner mind can take control of the muscles of your hand and can write intelligibly without your being aware of what it is writing. You can be reading a book while your hand writes. A few very good automatists have been able to read with the conscious mind while the right hand writes about something, and at the same time the left hand writes on some other subject. Thus, three different mental activities can be carried on at the same time! The operation of a Ouija board is just a variation of automatic writing.

The late Anita Mühl, an eminent psychiatrist, was our leading authority on this subject, with which she did much experimentation. She wrote a book, a classic in the field, called *Automatic Writing.** Dr. Mühl believed that four out of five people can learn to write automatically, though it may require several

* Reported by Leslie LeCron, in *How to Make the Next Ten Years the Best Years of Your Life* (West Nyack, N.Y.: Parker Publishing Co., Inc., 1966).

hours of training and practice to accomplish it. Those who doodle often can learn this ability, for doodling is the same type of activity. Doodles are meaningful if interpreted.

SIFTING GRAINS OF GOLD FROM THE SAND

As previously stated, the simplest device for testing your sensitivity in this area is the Ouija board. Many have made their own Ouija boards simply by writing all the letters of the alphabet across a flat surface, and under this all the numbers from one to nine (123456789), and perhaps the words "Yes" and "No," as on a real Ouija board. In this case, a pointer is not really needed. You merely close your eyes and let your finger move about the board of its own volition (apparently) and then see if what it spells out makes any sense. If you wish, you may use any smooth object that can slide around as a pointer, such as a drinking glass.

This was a parlor game that was very popular in the twenties, but many people grew tired of it because so much of what "came through" seemed to be gibberish. Of course it was gibberish; nine-tenths of what "comes through" even in the automatic speech and writing of trained mediums is gibberish. It takes patience and understanding to experiment with automatism, to sift the grains of gold from the sands of nonsense.

So, if you are patient, begin with the Ouija board and see what you can make out of it. Then, if you like, go on to automatic writing *without* the Ouija board.

SECRETS OF A SUCCESSFUL MEDIUM

It is not necessary to go into trance, or to be a medium in the usual sense, in order to write automatically. Some dissociation is usually present, however. This means that you are, temporarily, not concerned with and perhaps not even aware of your surroundings. We speak of someone's being "lost in thought"; such a person is really *dissociated* and, unlike the medium in trance or the person who has been hypnotized, can be *associated,* or brought back to awareness of the surroundings with a word, or by hearing a dog bark, or the ringing of a doorbell.

The first step in automatic writing is the achievement of this slight dissociation. Some people slip into it quite naturally just by thinking about it; others can induce it by concentrating attention on some object: a pencil, a ring, a glass, etc., until they feel relaxed and slightly sleepy. You may find that the necessary dissociation is present when you are half-awake, early in the morning or late at night.

When this dissociation is achieved, and you are relaxed, you will find that your mental processes, which you might think would be slowed down, are really accelerated. Words, ideas, phrases, whole sentences will flow through your mind, and with some effort you can rouse yourself enough to write them down. You may, in fact, become so tired of this unaccustomed flow of words that you will come fully awake, alert and irritable.

After writing down as best you can the words that rush through your mind, you will either come wide awake or go completely to sleep. No matter. If you have written down even a small part of what your stream of consciousness has produced, you will have an interesting record. You may need help to interpret it, and certainly most of it will be gibberish. But—if you are like most people who have tried this—there will be discernible in the gibberish ideas, phrases, and sentences that make sense; that, according to psychic research, *may not have originated in your own mind at all,* but in the mind of someone not in the body, who is taking advantage of your relaxed, receptive state and is trying to establish contact with you.

In his book *Immortality, the Scientific Evidence,** Alson J. Smith gives an illustration of this method:

* Alson J. Smith, *Immortality: the Scientific Evidence* (Englewood Cliffs, N.J.: Prentice-Hall, Inc., 1954).

"I am lying in bed at 5 A.M., brought half-awake by the sound of milk cans clattering on the pavement. My eyes are closed, but my mind is racing like a windmill. I am conscious of a vague orange light, but it is not yet dawn . . . The words, phrases, and sentences tumble through my mind, and 'something' says to me, 'Write it down.'

"By a great effort of will I reach the bedside table and get a paper and pencil. Heavily, reluctantly, almost painfully, I catch some of the racing words and, in the dark, write them down. I write like this for perhaps five minutes. Then I come fully awake and am aware of the first gray streaks of dawn and the dim outlines of objects in the room. My hand aches from the effort of writing, but, when I am fully awake, I am hardly conscious of having done any writing at all. The whole episode is fleeing backward in memory—but I have the record, the heavy scribblings on the piece of paper. It goes something like this:

> You were supposed but it didn't you know it isn't go go
>
> Where there is no night there now nor morning here if is in winter.
>
> But the school SCHOOL you never wanted and hurt on a nail.
>
> Like a ped remember and the ruler and the play money you didn't like it was Sylvia and the valentine but I sent you I sent you cried and all the games sister to New Street awful first time and the dog big dog you cut the lawn the little cards good fair bad all good blonde boy by the fire
>
> You said you hurt me on a nail I sent you through remember
>
> And the lunch always the condensed milk and cocoa the cereal lilac tree in the side yard but I sent you I sent you
>
> A ped a ped a foot and George George street of a kind and I sent you remember you hurt you on a nail I said it will feel better I sent you foot and George. . . .

"There was a lot more, but this was the only part of the record that made any sense at all to me. As a little boy I had attended a private school on George Street in Danbury, Connecticut, called 'Miss Foote's.' At this school we played 'store' with play-money and play-groceries, and on Valentine's Day a girl named Sylvia brought me a big lacey valentine. I would frequently try to evade school by alleging to my mother that 'I hurt me on a nail,' but she always sent me off anyway, saying it would feel better after a while. At school we would get little cards at the end of the day with a single word on them: Good, Fair, or Bad. When I came home for lunch, I would usually have cocoa with condensed milk in it and cereal. My sister had gone to New Street public school and had hated it because she had to pass a yard with a big dog tethered in it."

Was this, in truth, Mr. Smith's long-dead mother trying to identify herself? No one can categorically say so. But that is the way automatic writing works, and you can test your own ability at it, your own psychic sensitivity, in the same way.

AMATEURS WHO HAVE SUCCEEDED

Many of the outstanding automatists have been amateurs. One of the leading amateur automatists was Mrs. John H. Curran. Mrs. Curran was an average middle-class housewife, and had no particular interest in phychical phenomena. In the year 1913, however, the Ouija board was the latest "rage," and she, like a lot of other people, bought one. On a hot July evening, she and a friend, Mrs. Emily Grant Hutchings, were playing with the new toy at the Curran's home in St. Louis. They had "sat" with it before, but had never had any luck. On this particular evening (they were waiting for their husbands to come home), the little wooden pointer on the Ouija board began to move rapidly and definitely from one letter to another, spelling out a strange message:

> "Many moons ago I lived. Again I come. Patience Worth my name."

The women looked at each other in amazement. The pointer flew about the board again:

"Wait, I would speak with thee. If thou shalt live, then so shall I. I make my bread by thy hearth. Good friends, let us be merrie. The time for work is past. Let the tabbie drowse and blink her wisdom to the fire-log."

"How quaint!" exclaimed Mrs. Hutchings.

The board replied snappily:

"Good Mother wisdom is too harsh for thee and thou should'st love her only as a foster-mother."

That was the beginning of "Patience Worth." From then on, over a period of years, Patience poured a stream of communications through the Ouija board, operated by Mrs. Curran. There were epigrams, conversations, poems, stories, allegories—all in seventeenth-century English, all beautifully constructed and historically accurate. Two of the stories were actually published in novel form by Henry Holt and Co.

At first, it was believed that Patience Worth was really some part of the subconscious of Mrs. Hutchings, who was a writer of modest ability. However, it soon developed that it was Mrs. Curran, and not Mrs. Hutchings, through whom Patience was working. Patience was never in evidence unless Mrs. Curran was at the board, but Mrs. Hutchings' absence made no difference at all. As for Mrs. Curran, she had no literary pretensions, and only a cursory knowledge of English history.

HOW TO MAKE A SPIRIT LANTERN THAT LIGHTS UP THE INVISIBLE WORLD!

This method is recommended by Dr. L. W. de Laurence, in his book *India's Hood Unveiled* (de Laurence, Scott & Co., Chicago, 1910). It is a variation of the Lunar Circle and Psycho-Videoscope.

Take any ordinary, low voltage flashlight and remove the lens holder and the reflector. This will expose the bulb, which should give off a weak light without the reflector. The light must be weak. Check to make sure. Place the flashlight upended on a table or ledge that is high enough so that the light will be at about eye level when you sit down. Place a chair about an arm's length away, turn off all the lights so that the room is pitch dark, then turn on the flashlight.

Sit facing the light, with your feet resting squarely on the floor. Place your left thumb in the hollow of your right palm; close the fingers of your right hand over it. Rest your hands thus joined over the pit of your stomach. Relax your mind and body. Remain passive, gazing steadily at the light. Now begin breathing slowly and deeply for a period of thirty minutes. You will not at first be able to do this for thirty minutes but you may practice and lengthen the time by degrees.

After practicing the above exercise for a short time you should perceive a light blue-white aura above the halo of the light. As you continue to practice, this blue-white aura should become stronger and increase in lustre and area. At times the entire room may appear to light up, as if by lightning on a dark night. Again, you may observe a column of golden etheric waves passing before your eyes. Indeed there may appear several light waves of bright colors of the aura, such as blue, yellow, and red. Further, you may see a blue-white sparkling star-like light in glittering circles. These are manifestations of spirit or Astral lights which usually surround one when in the elementary stage of clairvoyance.

These spirit or Astral lights are likely to appear in any part of the room, and if your practicing is continued it is very likely that spirit faces will begin to materialize to you. It may be added, however, that many claim to get better and quicker results if a little temple incense is burned or some wax candles are used for a few minutes during the exercise. Mental requests should be thrown out and made for more spirit light and better materialization. Spirit faces appear only gradually at first, but in time they should become quite clear.

Continue your daily practice with earnestness and determination, and before long you will see the perfect form of a human spirit. You may speak to him (or her) mentally, and very probably you may notice a nodding of its head or a motion of its hands, in recognition of what you have said. At this stage, request earnestly that this spiritual being give you more light, and at once all necessary help will flow to you.

After you get a clear view of them, ask these spirit beings to move in different directions by means of mental commands. Some may and some may not respond to your commands. After a little while, however, you should see your wishes acted upon.

When you have developed to this stage, you may request the spirits to move any furniture from one place to another and do other things for you. In the course of time, you may request them to give you information on any subject.

Before this stage, and probably in the very early stages of this method, you may notice a noise like the "pop" or blast of a small pistol. If you hear such a noise, do not be afraid; such sounds, says Dr. de Laurence, are habitual before the appearance of spirit beings. If the noise becomes more audible, your clairaudient power is probably developing and after a time you will be able, through the aid of the spirit world, to hear whatever you want.

SUMMARY OF TELECULT POWER #8

1. A Magic Compass or Money Finder consists of any object, including the human hand, which a spirit may use to point to something, and thereby convey a message.
2. Spirit contact by means of an object that the spirit is asked to move is known as divination.
3. One remarkable form of divination is known as "dowsing." The "dowsing rod" is a kind of magic wand that acts as a directional compass. Anyone can try it, using a wire coat hanger, and following the directions in this chapter.

4. This device has been used by American marines in Vietnam to detect enemy tunnels.
5. Another device used for spirit contact, one which the spirits are asked to move, is a kind of "Magic Money Bag" known as an exploratory pendulum, which you may use to receive gifts from the invisible world. Gifts such as gold, silver, diamonds, platinum, and much more!
6. You may have a choice to make, or a problem that calls for knowledge that you do not possess. The inhabitants of the invisible world have access to all knowledge—past, present, and future. It is a simple matter to ask and receive answers with any of these devices.
7. Doctors have actually used the Magic Compass to successfully diagnose baffling cases. It has also been used with 90 percent accuracy to predict the sex of unborn children.
8. This chapter reveals a method by which you may actually receive Cosmic Letters from the invisible world, leading you to newfound treasures, such as money, love, success in business, the truth about others, and much more.
9. This chapter shows you how to make a Spirit Lantern that lights up the invisible world. This may be used in connection with your Psychic Tele-Viewer to see actual Photo-Forms (see Telecult Power #7).
10. By use of your mental Tele-Communicator, it is possible to ask the "little people" of the invisible world to move furniture or objects from one place to another, and do other things for you.

TELECULT POWER #9

HOW YOU CAN RECEIVE HELP FROM THE INVISIBLE WORLD

Throughout the mass of occult literature, there runs the legend of the Invisible Masters. This is said to be an organization of members of the spirit world, headed by the Ascended Masters and staffed with many devoted workers whose last earth lives were spent in study and earnest spiritual service to mankind. The express purpose of this organization is the upliftment of mankind and the furthering of its progress or evolution along spiritual lines.

Contact with the Invisible Masters can be most beneficial along material as well as spiritual lines. They are like Robert Louis Stevenson's "little people"—your invisible helpers. When you have identified these friends and clearly established your contact, you can expect tangible help of any sort you need.

HOW BEINGS FROM THE NEXT DIMENSION CAN HELP YOU

How can beings from the next dimension help you? Any way you can imagine, and a few ways known only to the spirits.

There is more truth than you might imagine to the old saying, "As you turn to God, God turns to you." What we are saying here is, "As you turn to the spirit world, it eagerly turns to you."

Beings from the next dimension have helped you many times in the past, although you were probably not aware of it.

A FLASH OF BLUE LIGHTNING SAVES HOLD-UP VICTIM!

In his book, *Helping Yourself with E.S.P.,** Al G. Manning tells about a middle-aged woman who was walking home from an evening church meeting. As she passed a tall hedge, she found herself looking right into the muzzle of a revolver. The voice said, "Let's have that purse," but it was interrupted by a flash of blue light like a tiny lightning bolt which knocked the gun to the pavement. The bandit fled in terror, and the woman hurried home in safety.

AN INVISIBLE HAND REACHED OUT AND SAVED HIM!

Mr. Manning relates how, in another instance, a young boy was swimming alone in a secluded bay. As often is the case for young boys, he overestimated his prowess and soon found himself over his head and sinking from panic and exhaustion. Suddenly a hand grabbed his trunks and lifted him just out of the water. He was transported in this fashion back to where the water came up only to his waist, and deposited back on his feet by the invisible hand.†

---

* Al G. Manning, *Helping Yourself with E.S.P.* (West Nyack, N.Y.: Parker Publishing Co., Inc., 1966).

† *Ibid.*

SPIRIT HELP IN FINDING MONEY

In his book, *The Amazing Laws of Cosmic Mind Power*,* Dr. Joseph Murphy tells how, some years ago, a girl named Anne, whom he had never met, phoned him, saying, "My father died. I know he has hidden a large sum of money in the house. I am panic-sticken, desperate, and full of fear; I need the money and I can't find it."

Dr. Murphy told her he would pray about it, and that night he had a dream in which a man said, "Get up and write this down." Dr. Murphy sleepily awoke, went to his desk, and rustled through the drawer for a sheet of paper. The voice of the man in the dream dictated to him as he wrote.

Dr. Murphy says, "I am sure that these instructions were not written by me alone—or even by my subconscious in the half-dream world in which I was. I definitely feel that it was the personality of the father of the girl, surviving so-called death, who gave me the instructions which explained in detail where a large sum of money was hidden, with explicit instructions to his daughter whom to contact, etc. All of this was subsequently verified."

A VISION OF GOLD

People have visions of great wealth every day. But seldom are they so specific as to enable one to actually cash in! Nevertheless, that is exactly what happened to Mrs. Helen W., of Phoenix, Arizona.

Mrs. W. dreamt of an abandoned house in her vicinity. In this dream, something whispered to her, "Go to this house. There is rich gold there."

Knowing the area quite well, she climbed up a hill to inspect

* Joseph Murphy, *The Amazing Laws of Cosmic Mind Power* (West Nyack, N.Y.: Parker Publishing Co., Inc., 1965).

the abandoned dwelling. Carefully examining the walls in the places where the plaster had fallen off, Mrs. W. found solid gold. The walls were made with bricks of solid gold!

THE MAN WHO MADE A FORTUNE WITH TELECULT POWER

Years ago, a man named Armand V. Hasen used Telecult Power to actually "break the bank" at Monte Carlo. Using the power this book gives you, he could forecast the run of the bobbing roulette ball, the progress of a horse race, the sequence of a deck of cards. He could stand by a roulette wheel and tell roughly nine times out of ten whether the wheel would come up red or black, and about twice a night the exact number which would win flashed across his Psychic Tele-Viewer.

After a week, and with a fortune in his bank account, Armand V. Hasen called it quits, and has spent the rest of his life using this power to help others.

* * *

If spirits can influence the movement of a pendulum or a divining rod, why not the fall of a pair of dice, or the number that comes up on a roulette wheel? That is a theory that many subscribe to as a probable explanation for this and the phenomena cited in the section "Your Mental Levitating Finger."

PENNIES FROM HEAVEN

Recently it was reported * that near Bristol, England, a five-year-old girl was returning from school when some pennies rained out of the sky at her feet. As she stooped to pick them up another handful came showering down.

The girl, of course, had to tell her friends at school, and the

* Reported by Michael Hervey in *Strange Happenings* (New York: Ace Star Books, 1966).

next day they all trooped to the "Pennies from Heaven Street." Pennies started to rain down within a few seconds of their arrival.

Today, children from every corner of the town converge upon Westfield Close every day, but there are always enough coins to go around, literally thousands of them being picked up, many of them in less than an hour!

HOW YOU MAY RECEIVE HELP FROM YOUR SPIRIT DOCTORS

Probably one of the most remarkable examples of how spirit doctors work, is the story of Edgar Cayce. Cayce was born in Kentucky in 1876, and had little education. When he was twenty-one, a hypnotist named Layne cured him of what seemed a permanent loss of voice.

While Cayce was under hypnosis, his frequent use of the word "we see" suggested he was receiving help from invisible beings of some sort. *He* told the doctor what to do.

On awakening, Cayce found himself cured, and was then persuaded by Layne to let himself be hypnotized again so that he, or those behind him, could diagnose Layne's own stomach trouble. Cayce, in hypnosis, not only did so, but prescribed a treatment which completely cured him.

After that, rather reluctantly, Cayce consented to let himself be hypnotized so that he could diagnose and prescribe for other people. After a number of cures had been effected, the news reached a man named Dr. Hugo Munsterberg of Harvard University, an arch exposer of quacks and spiritualists. It took him exactly three days to admit that Cayce was no fraud.

From that time until his death in 1944, Cayce devoted his life to helping people through information received from his spirit teachers and doctors. He soon learned to hypnotize himself to make contact. He charged no fees, but accepted free-will offerings from those who wished to give.

At one point, when Cayce's wife was desperately ill with tuberculosis, a doctor assured him that he had better try his hand, for his wife was past human help. He also agreed to the drastic remedies which Cayce—or his voices—prescribed in sleep. Mrs. Cayce completely recovered.

On another occasion Cayce's son, Hugh Lynn Cayce, burned his eyes with some flash powder. The doctors were convinced that his sight was destroyed and wanted to remove one eye "to save the boy's life."

Cayce went into a trance and prescribed tannic acid to be added to the bandages. The doctors were certain that it would be too strong, but as they were equally sure the sight was gone they agreed. On the sixteenth morning the bandages were removed. Hugh Lynn could see as well as before the accident.

SUMMARY OF TELECULT POWER #9

1. Throughout the mass of occult literature, there runs the legend of the Invisible Masters. This is said to be an organization of members of the spirit world devoted to helping the living.
2. Contact with the Invisible Masters can be most beneficial along material as well as spiritual lines. When you have identified these friends and clearly established your contact, you can expect tangible help of any sort you need.
3. These invisible helpers have helped you many times in the past, although you were probably not aware of it.
4. In times of emergency, your friends in the next dimension can act as invisible bodyguards.
5. These invisible beings can diagnose ailments and even prescribe miraculous remedies beyond the knowledge of human beings.
6. These invisible beings can lead you to hidden treasures, such as a will hidden in the lining of an old coat, money in cash,

stocks and bonds hidden under floor boards or buried under the ground; solid gold bricks sealed in a wall; as well as treasures in other places.

7. They can help you win money in games of chance by telling you in advance where a roulette ball will land, which horse will win a race, and much more.
8. They can even drop actual money from the sky.

TELECULT POWER #10

HOW TO RECOGNIZE COSMIC SIGNS

If you have been reading these pages faithfully, you have seen how easy it is to come into contact with the spirit helpers. You have received amazing evidence that these helpers really exist.

By means of Telecult Power, you were able to come into direct contact with them and receive answers to your questions! You have also seen how they try to arrange circumstances in your favor—even if you deny their existence and spurn their help.

> **In this chapter you shall see how to recognize this help in your everyday life—in the form of signs or suggestions. These signs can take the form of dreams, omens, apparitions, feelings, natural phenomena, what other people say or do, even the behavior of animals. Spirit signs always point the way to opportunities, which if acted upon literally push you ahead to success with little or no effort.**

It's like "power steering." When an automobile is so equipped, one touch of a finger can accomplish what it took two hands to accomplish before. In the same way, when you are in harmony with the spirit world, everything is easy.

In the next few pages, we shall see some of the ways the spirit helpers reveal their signs to you. While it is not possible to predict the exact sign that will be revealed in a given situation, most cosmic signs and the circumstances under which they are revealed do have certain specific characteristics which it is possible to talk about. These include:

1. The Signs of Love
2. The Signs of Prosperity
3. The Signs of Right
4. The Signs of Wrong
5. The Signs of Danger
6. The Signs of Salvation

We will talk about each of these types of signs, in the light of specific facts which have been gathered over the years from the lives and actual accounts of men and women in all walks of life. Then, perhaps, it will be easier for you to recognize these signs in your own life.

STEP ONE: HOW INVISIBLE SIGNS BECOME VISIBLE

Every day you receive signs from the spirits. If you would but heed these signs, your life would be a heaven on earth. They send you signs that tell you exactly what to do to make your loved ones more responsive. They send you signs that tell you when you are in the company of someone who is deeply attracted to you—despite what he or she might say. They send you signs to let you know whether those you deal with are being honest and sincere with you. They warn you of danger long before it comes to pass. Should you have any pressing problem—such as where to find the money you need, what to do to get out of an embarrassing situation, how to fulfill some long-felt desire, *there are signs.*

All day long, you are being literally bombarded with wonderful, magical, transforming signs, lovingly sent to you by spirit helpers. As you sit reading this now, wondering how you are ever going to realize those dreams you have, how you are ever going to find that doctor who can help you, how you are ever going to locate that long-lost friend or relative, how you are ever going to lay your hands on the money you need to get out of that neighborhood and into a better one, how you are ever going to avoid the misfortune that you have reason to believe is in store for you (or do this for a friend or relative) . . .

> **For each and every one of these question marks in your mind there is an answer, a SIGN—invisible to you now—but clear as life and plain as day when you take one simple step.**

And the first giant step in recognizing these cosmic signs is simply to admit the possibility that they come; to admit the possibility that there is a Divine Intelligence in this Universe that works in mysterious ways, beyond our comprehension, to help us. An Intelligence that is aware of the difficulties we face, a Power so big we can't see it. Who gave us free will—because He'd rather have us know and like Him freely than have to seize our minds and say: "Look here, you're going to love me, or else!"

STEP TWO: THE TIMING OF A SIGN

The next step is to realize that no matter how this Master Mind chooses to reveal a sign to you, it will invariably be the one most appropriate to the occasion, and most easily recognizable to you.

If, for example, the occasion calls for quick action, no matter how baffling the problem, there is always a sign at that instant to tell you what to do. If, on the other hand, the situation calls for no immediate action, the sign may come at any time—within the interval of a few hours, or perhaps days. Yet it *always* comes.

STEP THREE: WHAT TO DO WHEN YOU RECEIVE A SIGN

This is the easiest step of all. Do exactly what the sign tells you to do. Act on it—remembering always that the Master Mind's signs are like "power steering." They always point the way to opportunities, which if acted upon, literally push you ahead to success with little or no effort.

HOW TO DEAL WITH THE DEVIL

One thing must be made clear. A sign from the Master Mind is a message. Whether you recognize this message depends, to a great extent, on your frame of mind. Satan thrives on disbelief. Nothing catches his attention faster than when you doubt, disbelieve, or continually look on the gloomy side of things. When you do this, he appears at your side in a flash, feeding more and more evil thoughts into your mind, increasing each doubt and each complaint, and actually blocks or distorts the Master Mind's message to you.

> **There is only one way to defeat Satan, and this is to believe. The Master Mind does not ask you to believe in Him right away—but for your own sake He does ask you to believe, at least, in the possibility of ultimate good. In other words, try to look on the bright side of things. Try to see the good in every situation, tell yourself always that no matter how bad things look, they can get better.**

As soon as you do this, a world of wonder and beauty and golden opportunities opens before you. And it becomes a very simple matter, indeed, to see the Master Mind's signs.

Let's see how this works in actual practice!

COSMIC SIGN REVEALS A $25,000 INCOME!

Two artists once opened up a shop together, doing any kind of work they could get. One noticed that whenever he happened to do portraits for people, the results were so effective that they came back for more. Concentrating on portraits, he was soon earning $25,000 a year—while his partner was still struggling to make a living. That's how simple it is to recognize a sign straight from the vast cosmos above! Everybody does at least one good thing well. You may not realize it, but you, too, have a hidden talent. Watch for it. Listen to what other people say about you. Then proceed to cash in on it.

COSMIC SIGN REVEALS A RICH OIL FIELD

Recently, a Tennessee farmer who was just barely making ends meet was idly inspecting his fields. As he came to a small stream, where the cattle came to drink, he noticed a wooden board that had been placed across it. The board seemed to be holding back a kind of scum that was carried by the water's current. He knelt and dabbed at it with his finger. It smelled like oil. So he had some experts come out and check. It turned out to be one of the richest oil fields in the country.

What riches, what opportunities, are you overlooking?

SIGN REVEALS POT OF GOLD!

The following is an old English folk-tale that is told in connection with a statue of one John Chapman, in Swaffham, England.

John Chapman made a poor living as a blacksmith in the town of Swaffham, until he had his dream which told him to go to London where he would meet a man on London Bridge who would make his fortune for him.

Imagine Mrs. Chapman's scolding at her husband's stupidity in making a hundred-mile journey on account of a dream! Nevertheless, he went.

For the next three days and nights he hung about on London Bridge. Not a soul spoke to him. He was just about to skulk home, ashamed, to meet the reproaches of his wife when a man who kept a shop on the Bridge accosted him and asked curiously why he had been hanging around. John told him.

The man roared with laughter that anyone should act so stupidly on account of a dream.

"If I were foolish enough to take any notice of dreams," he said, "I should now be at a place called Swaffham, where I dreamed one John Chapman has a tree in his back garden with a pot of money under it!"

It only remains to say that the shopkeeper was wrong. There were two pots!

This is not to say that you should act on *all* dreams. Some dreams are caused by events that happened fleetingly the day before, and your dream is simply a more lingering reflection on them. There is also the "surface" dream, which is caused by too much to eat or a crease in the sheet. Do not waste your time over these. We shall have more to say about dreams later on in this chapter.

THE SIGN OF LOVE

You may think that this is a difficult type of sign to recognize. Actually, it is the easiest of them all, because Love is and always has been the original, basic, and strongest life force.

God lovingly created man, hoping that man would return that love. How is that love best returned? *By loving life*—and, realizing that God is in everything, by loving all of His creations. And what is God's most miraculous creation? Why, man himself, of course! ("Created He him in His image.") Love, then, is blessed! All forms of love: friendship, admiration, passion, awe.

It is the Master Mind's *will,* pulsating, throbbing within us, urging, imploring. We need not obey. Over the years we can build up many mental barriers to love, if we want to, since He gave us free will. But the love that we are capable of, the love God wants us to show, is always there.

HOW TO SEE PEOPLE AND EVENTS IN YOUR FUTURE WITH THE AMAZING PSYCHO-VIDEOSCOPE!

To perceive the signs of love in your everyday life, try this form of Telecult Vision, which involves the seeing or revelation to you of forthcoming events. The whole process is based on the fact that Cosmic Intelligence tries to arrange circumstances in your favor.

To this extent, your future *is* predetermined. Events will occur in your life, *as planned* by the Cosmic Intelligence over which you have no control. This means that certain people, places and events are moving toward you—or you toward them —aside from, and far in advance of any plans you may be even vaguely considering. Opportunities for love, prosperity, and happiness will be presented to you. You have but to recognize and act on them.

This technique, which is a kind of Mirrorscope or Telephoto-Transmitter (see Telecult Power #2), increases the power of your mental television. All you need is a Bible, an oil lamp, a mirror and a glass of water from a sunrise spring. A sunrise spring is a spring that faces east.

Place the Bible on a table, with the glass of water on top of it. Behind the glass, or to the right of it, place a low voltage lamp (an oil lamp will do). Seating yourself with your back to the table, and a little to the left of the glass of water, hold a mirror up in front of you.

Make sure the room is quiet and free of distractions, otherwise it will be impossible to receive this mysterious telecast.

Look directly into the mirror, concentrating on the reflected light. Seat yourself in a comfortable position when you do this, as it may be quite a while before you see anything. Above all, be patient.

Eventually you will see an image in the reflected light. It may be some person, place or thing which will some day have a direct bearing on your life. The images will stay in your mirror until you have seen all there is to see.

One man, who reports that his mother told him about this method when he was a child, says he used it to see his future wife, and that he has also seen in it the faces of other persons who have come into his life, as well as his present business and the little home in which he raised his family.

A MAGIC RING THAT LETS YOU TALK WITH ANIMALS

It is said that Solomon was the wisest man of his time and possibly of all time. Few things were mysteries to him and he is supposed to have possessed many remarkable powers. One of these was the ability to "talk" to animals.

To do this, he used a special ring, which he put on his right index finger. Magic power was contained in the ring and the animals knew it. In reality, the magic ring that lets you talk with animals is the golden ring of human love and understanding.

SIGNS OF DANGER

Animals, whose minds are free of the complicated patterns of human thought, are the perfect receivers of the Master Mind's signs and manifestations. To begin with, animals always seem to sense the presence of "ghosts" or invisible beings. When such a spectre is evil, animals have been known to go mad with fright. Animals are also the first to know when danger or death is imminent and try to warn us of the fact.

SIGN OF SALVATION

A classic example of this type of rescue story comes from Wales. Maggie T. had quarreled with her financé, Jim, a fisherman. That night a violent storm blew up and Jim did not return to shore. Maggie sat up all night, waiting for "a sign," as she put it. Suddenly her cat seemed to go mad. It clawed at Maggie's dress, dragging her toward the door.

It led her down to the beach where the waves had deposited a body. It was Jim, just barely alive.

* * *

From Canada comes another example of an animal sensing danger. A man tried to make his horse cross a bridge. It refused to move. A few minutes later the bridge collapsed for no apparent reason.

SIGN OF RICHES

A Pekingese's occult powers have been put to good use by its owner, an Englishwoman. She shows her pet a list of horses running that day and the dog points out his choice with his paw. According to the newspapers he has helped his owner win a small fortune.

SIGN OF REUNION

A heavy storm marooned Mrs. Albert H., of Gary, Indiana in a small town in Ohio. While waiting in a restaurant for the storm to abate, Mrs. H. happened to mention her long lost brother to the restaurant owner. The restaurant owner tipped her off to a woman, who turned out to be her sister-in-law, and through her she was reunited with her brother, whom she hadn't seen in 28 years.

YOU CAN HEAR GOD'S VOICE

Each and every day the Master Mind makes His will known to you in a dozen different ways. And yet these signs are apparent to you only if you earnestly try to see them. Even before this can happen you need a basic kind of faith.

In these chapters we have tried to help strengthen your faith. If you have followed the simple methods and procedures outlined, you must already have had many overwhelming indications in your life that the Master Mind really exists.

If you have followed the methods of prayer, for example, I know that help has come in some form. If it has not entirely materialized, the one sure way to tell if it is on its way is if things are gradually becoming clearer to you.

The more you use these methods—the methods for asking questions and receiving answers for example—the better they work, and the greater your faith. It's easy to believe when you receive!

By the same token, God's will is no more than the easier of two paths. It may come to you in the form of a dream, an occurrence, or a remark that someone makes. In many instances, all that is required of you to receive His signs is a keen sense of awareness, as in the story about the Tennessee farmer who found oil.

With these techniques, your sensitivity to cosmic signs and manifestations may reach such heights that you may actually hear the Cosmic Voice that travels a million light-years through time and space. It can happen! Or you may hear the voice of one of His spirit agents.

DREAMS, SIGNS AND OMENS

Who has not wondered what the future holds for him? Could he but know that the road ahead is paved with gold, how reassuring it would be! If, on the other hand, his path were wrong, would it not be prudent to seek another route?

Each of us must make many choices in the course of a lifetime. We ponder which path to take—which trade to learn, which job to choose, which house to buy, which mate to wed, which doctor to trust. We yearn for some reliable advisor to tell us when to go, where to turn, and in whom to confide.

Yet isn't the Master Mind just such an advisor? And if history tells us anything, it is that His advice is certainly reliable! One of the ways this Master Mind advises us is in dreams.

Dreams are our link with the nether world of the spirit, where cosmic influences are brought to bear in their purest form. In dreams, you can converse with departed loved ones. In dreams, you can take fantastic astral journeys into the dimensions of the past, the present, and the future. In dreams, the Master Mind can communicate with you.

"Let me produce the state of sleep," said the philosopher Josephus, in the First Century, A.D., "as a most evident demonstration of the truth of what I say, wherein souls, when the body does not distract them, have the sweetest rest depending on themselves, and conversing with God, by their alliance with him; they then go everywhere, and foretell many futurities beforehand."

"It seems strange how much there is about dreams in the Bible," observed Abraham Lincoln. "There are sixteen chapters in the Old Testament and four or five in the New in which dreams are mentioned, and there are many other passages through the Bible which refer to visions. If we believe the Bible, we must accept the fact that many things are made known in our dreams."

Even in our own day, Freud has written: "(It has always appeared to people) that dreams serve a special purpose in respect to the dreamer . . . that, as a rule, they predict the future. . . . The ancients distinguished between the true and valuable dreams which were sent to the dreamer as warnings, or to foretell future events."

• • •

In these pages we have seen many examples of the valuable information that can be received through dreams. Each dream was a clear revelation of the message being sent. But by far the greater number of dreams that we have are not so clear in meaning. There is a good reason for this. All dreams are a form of telepathy, which means—literally—communication at a distance, in time or space—or both.

Peripheral vision and peripheral hearing (mentioned in Telecult Power #2) are a simple form of distance communication. A sight or sound not consciously perceived by you three days ago, because your attention was fixed on something else at the time, *was* actually received by you and passed directly into your subconscious mind. Now, three days later, when your conscious mind is not busily engaged in other matters, this memory pops into your mind. You may vaguely recall the circumstances, or it may come as a complete surprise to you.

Another example of distance communication is the "delayed reaction" often experienced by persons in mind-to-mind contact. If you are close to some person, or have been working telepathically with him, he may send you a message at a time not previously arranged. You may be involved in some work at the time, and your attention completely focused on what you are doing. In such cases the message may be properly received and stored, then released at a later time when your conscious mind is at rest.

A third example of delayed communication is spirit contact. Like all forms of telepathy, a message so received passes directly to your subconscious mind, which throws it up to your conscious mind. There it is received, provided the conscious mind is at rest.

Confusion arises when only a partial message is received, or when a person does not know he has received a message from outside. In such cases, he thinks this impression is his own. He does not know why he received it, and in the absence of reason, emotion prevails in his mind.

For example, a sender may project the word "hurry," or "make haste," having in mind nothing more than that the person in front of him should hurry up and make his purchase so that he can get finished. The receiver, however, does not know this. Even though he correctly receives the idea of "make haste," he becomes confused, and starts to surround it with all sorts of dire emotional pictures. To quote a student of these matters, Joseph J. Weed: "He will experience a sense of frustration because he is not proceeding faster. He will fear he is failing because he is not fast enough. He will feel resentment at the circumstances which he believes retard his progress. In short, he will find himself in a complete emotional turmoil because of the implied urgency in the message 'make haste.'" *

But the state of mind in which emotion is most likely to prevail is in sleep, when the conscious mind is temporarily "tuned off" or out of touch with the outside world. It is then that a host of memories—including delayed memories, and messages from unknown sources—become intertwined and impossible to ferret out, except by the means indicated in Telecult Power #8, (automatic speech and automatic writing).

Every dream, in other words, can contain two kinds of messages. The first type are messages originating from outside the mind. The second type are your emotional responses to that message.

This second type of message indicates your particular pattern of thinking at the time: hidden, unconscious thoughts in your mind that are pushing up to the level of consciousness, and may soon be influencing your actions.

---

* Joseph J. Weed, *Wisdom of the Mystic Masters* (West Nyack, N.Y.: Parker Publishing Co., Inc., 1968).

Psychologists have discovered that similar dreams tend to occur in the minds of most people, and that the second—or emotional—part of these messages tends to have the same or similar meaning. For your convenience, here is a list of—

500 DREAMS REVEALED!

Abundance ....Desire for independence.
Accident ....Desire to end friendship; warning of impending illness.
Accordion ....To hear, a disappointment; to play, happiness.
Accounting ....Desire for advancement; also, confusion.
Accusations ......Suspicion.
Acrobat ....The scheme you are considering is dangerous.
Actor, actress .....Desire for recognition.
Addition ....Many worries.
Admiral ....Desire for power.
Adultery ....Guilt complex, involving sexual relationship.
Agony ....Sign of approaching illness; fear or jealousy.
Airplane ....Desire for escape.
Alley ....Symbol of sexual desire.
Alligator ....Danger.
Altar ....Reminder about something unsatisfactory.
Anchor ....Desire for permanent home or occupation.
Angel ....Unexpected blessings; news of marriage; sign of protection from harm.
Animals ....If wild, lust for sex. If docile, contentment.
Ants ....Petty annoyances.
Ape ....Suspicion of friend.
Apples ....Sex urge.
Arrow ....Non-Freudian interpretation: symbol of festivity.

Attorney ....Difficulties seen ahead.
Auction ....Worry about business.
Automobile ....Desire for escape, financial gain, sex.
Ax ....Desire for advancement.
Baby ....Crying, disappointment. Laughing, contentment. Sleeping, desire for a mate. Nursing, a sign of deception by some acquaintance.
Ball ....To dream of going to one, ambition.
Ballet ....Infidelity, jealousy, possible quarrels.
Balloon ....Desire for escape.
Banana ....If overripe, boredom with work or partner.
Bandit ....Suspicion of associates.
Bar, bartender ....Desire for escape from responsibilities.
Barber ....Confusion in love or money.
Baseball ....Desire for harmony.
Basket ....Full, good fortune. Empty, misfortune.
Basketball ....See "Baseball."
Bath ....Interest in opposite sex; guilt complex.
Bats ....Worry over possible bad news.
Battle ....Frustration.
Bayonet ....Fear of some person, place or thing.
Beach ....Need for relaxation; sex desire.
Beads ....To wear, need for attention. To string, much work ahead.
Bear ....Threat of a rival.
Bed ....Other than your own, new opportunities. To make your bed signifies making new friends.
Bedroom ....Sex urge.
Bees ....Attention to business.
Beggar ....To give, self-deception. To see one, portends possible loss. To refuse to give, check finances.

Bells .... Possible death of friend; perplexing problem.
Berries .... To eat, loss of money, possible illness.
Betting .... Indicates speculation in real life.
Bicycle .... To ride downhill warns of possible misfortune.
Bigamist .... Jealousy, suspicion.
Billiards .... Trouble.
Birds .... If on perch, contentment. If singing or wounded, sadness. Talking, gossip.
Bird's nest .... If empty, gloom. If full, good business opportunities seen.
Blind .... To be blind, desire to escape reality. To see a blind person means someone you know needs help.
Blindman's bluff ... Loss of money, humiliation, through foolishness.
Birthday .... Optimism.
Blossom .... Growing or gather, happiness. Withered, sadness.
Boa constrictor .... Danger perceived.
Boat .... Desire for escape; sex urge.
Bomb .... Emotional distress.
Book(s) .... Cultural interest; need for more work; lack of knowledge.
Bookkeeper .... See "Accounting."
Boots .... Perception of changes taking place in one's life.
Boss .... Pleasant or unpleasant dream about, reflects real life situation.
Bottles .... If filled, outlook good. If empty, outlook dim.
Bouquet .... See "Blossom."
Bow and arrow ... Desire to be self-reliant. If arrow misses, disappointment in business or love.

Bowling ....See "Baseball."
Box ....If empty, frustration. If filled, plans for travel. If filled with money or jewels, outlook good. Sex symbol.
Boxing ....Unpredictable worries.
Bracelet ....Sign of marriage, indiscretion, perplexing situation. If found, good luck.
Bread ....Sign of good luck. If stale, bad omen.
Breakfast ....Loss of energy, depression, worries.
Bride ....A sign of good fortune, but may also indicate jealousy.
Bridge ....Crossing, overcoming difficulties.
Broom ....Sense of thrift; desire for improvement.
Brush ....Warns dreamer about carelessness.
Bug(s) ....Petty annoyances.
Bugle ....To hear, good sign. To blow, a warning.
Buildings ....New buildings, good opportunities seen. Old buildings, threat of failure.
Bull ....For a man, competition in business. For a woman, romance. Also a sign of money.
Burglar ....See "Bandit."
Burial ....Subconscious dissatisfaction with someone close. One's own burial signifies frustration.
Butterflies ....Optimism, good news ahead.
Buttons ....Lost, anxiety over money; found, expectation of gain.
Cab ....Secretiveness.
Cabin ....Good luck after much work. Ship's cabin, a warning of enemies.
Cage ....See "Birds," "Box."
Cakes ....Desire to socialize.
Calendar ....Warning about carelessness.
Camera ....Desire for change; signs of change. For woman, very pleasant experience with male companion.

Camping .... Desire to escape.
Candles .... Burning steadily, constancy.
Candlestick ...... With candle, happiness. Without, sadness.
Candy .... To receive, outlook good. To give, disappointment.
Cane .... To carry, a sign of confidence and good luck. To drop or break, the opposite.
Cannibal .... Fear.
Cannon .... Warning of struggles ahead.
Canoe .... To paddle your own indicates desire to be self-reliant. In rough waters, discontent. In calm waters, happiness.
Cap .... Desire to socialize.
Cape .... Signifies authority.
Captain .... Noble aspirations.
Car .... See "Automobile."
Cardinal .... To see an official of the church shows a desire to overcome wrong, to gain strength.
Cards .... Denotes desire to succeed.
Carnival .... Foretells a period of changes.
Carpenter .... Denotes need for diligent work.
Carpet .... To clean, warns of need to attend to personal affairs. Walking on, portends luxurious living.
Carrots .... Outlook good.
Castle .... Great ambitions.
Cat .... Symbol of woman.
Cave .... You are faced with many dilemmas. Sexual implications.
Cellar .... Lack of self-confidence.
Cemetery .... Predicts news from someone long absent.
Chair .... Indicates obligations you must meet. May portend illness for person sitting in it.
Champion .... Ambition.
Checkers .... Ambition.

Cheese ....Stubbornness.
Cherries ....Outlook good.
Chess or checkers ..Difficulties that must be resolved.
Chickens ....Need for planning.
Children ....If happy, good sign. If ill, money troubles.
Choking ....If being choked, fear of someone in real life. If choking another, hatred of that person.
Church ....Hopes yet to be fulfilled.
Clergy ....See "Cardinal."
Climbing ....Overcoming obstacles, but eventual success.
Clock ....Fear of loss of time. To see the clock, fear of loss of job or status. To hear it, fear of death to self or someone else.
Clouds ....Portend troublesome times.
Coat ....If new, desire for honors. If borrowed, you will borrow from that person. If lost, avoid speculations.
Cock ....To here cock crow in morning, good sign.
Cocktails ....Warning to refrain from exaggerating.
Coffee klatch .....Warning about gossip.
Coffin ....Bad luck.
Coins ....Dull silver, unhappiness. Bright gold or silver, bright opportunities.
Collar ....If tight, you mistrust someone.
College ....Ambition.
Comb ....To dream of combing, forebodes illness.
Compass ....Prosperity with the help of others.
Concert ....Need for recognition.
Confetti ....Desire for happiness.
Conjuror ....Suspicion of deceit; desire to be admired.
Convent ....Desire for escape from reality; for girl, disillusionment, despair.
Convention ....Portends increase in finances.

Cooking ....To cook, desire to make someone happy. To see cooking, gossip.
Corpse ....Finality, failure, desire for escape or forgiveness.
Cradle ....Sense of insecurity.
Criminal ....See "Bandit."
Crying ....Sorrow in love or business.
Curtains ....Threatens illness, embarrassment.
Cutting ....Emotional fear, distrust, desire to sever relationship or escape unpleasant situation.
Dagger ....Anxiety, fear of bodily injury; desire for sexual relationship that might harm you morally. Male sex symbol.
Daisy ....Love, good health.
Dancing ....Happiness. Sexual urge.
Death ....See "Corpse."
Dentist ....Suspicion of friend.
Desert ....Desire to rehabilitate one's self.
Detective ....See "Police."
Devil ....Susceptibility to flattery and temptation.
Diamond ....Good omen.
Dinner ....See "Breakfast."
Ditch ....To fall in one portends loss of integrity. To jump over indicates a narrow escape from this.
Divorce ....Marriage needs mending.
Doctor ....Dreamer has a discouraging situation and is seeking help subconsciously.
Dogs ....To hear a dog baying, separation from loved ones. A growling dog, resentment. Police dogs, fear, guilt, desire for protection.
Doll ....For child, loneliness. For adult, desire to be protected.

Dominoes ....To play, a desire for adulation.
Donkey ....To lead a donkey, a feeling of oppression. To ride, sex urge. To fall or be kicked by, indicates a feeling of unluckiness that is only in the dream.
Door ....Fear of loss of money.
Drinking ....See "Bar, bartender."
Driving ....Desire for independence, escape.
Drowning ....Desire to be reborn.
Dwarf ....Feeling of inadequacy, helplessness.
Dying ....If you are dying, it is a sense of guilt. If you see someone else dying, it is a desire to remove all authority from that person.
Eagle ....High ambitions, desire for fame and recognition.
Eating ....See "Breakfast."
Elephant ....Desire to have great strength, perhaps sexual.
Elevator ....Going up, feeling of advancement. Going down, bad luck.
Embrace ....A longing to help others.
Employer ....See "Boss."
Engine, engineer ..Wish to demonstrate power.
Escalator ....See "Elevator."
Escape ....Desire for escape.
Eve ....Temptation.
Execution ....Guilty feelings. If you are the executioner, desire to overthrow someone in authority.
Falling ....Symbol of fear, failure in work or home life.
Fan ....Symbol of vanity, rivalry.
Farm ....Desire for security and peace of mind.
Father ....Symbol of dominance, authority.
Fear ....Refers to conscious fears.
Fence ....To be encircled by, means that you are restraining yourself. For woman, it symbolizes desire for marriage.

Fighting ....The will to succeed despite many handicaps.
Fire ....Desire for escape, "burning your bridges," one might say.
Fish ....The fish is the symbol of life. A dead fish warns of losses. Fishing, a sign of good luck.
Flying ....Feeling of achievement, ambition. Flying low presents problems.
Forest ....If you are alone and happy, a wish to find a new home. Falling leaves, bad news.
Flag ....Peace of mind. A flag in the breeze is a warning to relax.
Flame ....See "Candles," "Fire."
Flies ....See "Ants."
Floating ....Unresolved problems.
Floods ....Warning to take care; success after hard work.
Flowers ....See "Blossom."
Flute ....Desire for friends, recognition.
Football ....See "Baseball."
Fox ....Suspicions.
Frogs ....Symbol of good luck, good health.
Fruit ....Sign of uncertainty in business affairs. Green fruit is a warning against haste.
Funeral ....See "Cemetery."
Gambling ....You are prone to gamble in everyday life.
Games ....See "Baseball."
Gang ....See "Bandit."
Garden ....See "Blossom."
Gate ....Closed, portends difficulties. Broken, sense of failure.
Ghost ....If the ghost has a resemblance to a parent, it is a warning of danger.
Gift ....If you dream that you receive a gift, check your finances for any discrepancy. To send a gift indicates desire for attention, flattery.

Gloves ....Warning to be economical, beware of deceit. If you find a pair of gloves, look for a new interest.

Goat ....A symbol of male potency, authority.

Gold ....To find is a symbol of ambition. To touch is a good omen.

Grapes ....Portend hardships.

Grass ....Smooth, green grass symbolizes happiness and peace of mind.

Grave ....To dig is to try to avoid punishment. To bury someone indicates argument.

Gun ....Warning to guard against mismanagement, dishonor.

Gutter ....Symbolizes immorality.

Gypsy ....Indicates wish for change of fortune.

Hair ....To comb your hair foretells of worries induced by generosity. Loss of hair, lack of sexual fulfillment.

Hammer ....Forebodes economic obstacles.

Hand ....Beautiful hands, desire for distinction. A hand with no body, arguments with family. Holding hands, emotional strain. Hairy hands, sexual fantasies.

Handcuffs ....Rigid ties that are unbearable to you.

Harp ....Bad luck.

Hat ....New hat, change of location. Loss, bad luck.

Holiday ....Feeling of optimism; good luck.

Horse ....Escape, ambition, sexual desire.

Hospital ....Fear of confinement, concern with health, feeling of helplessness.

Hotel ....Desire for change of home or occupation.

House ....Building new house, change in plans. See "Buildings."

Husband ....For unmarried woman, desire to be married. For married woman, some emotional conflict in marriage.

Ice ....Sign of actual physical discomfort. Floating on, jealousy. Walking on, danger.

Insects ....See "Ants."

Island ....Desire for escape from present circumstances.

Jail, jailer ....Small worries, desire to escape, guilt feelings.

Jewelry ....Fine jewelry, high ambitions. Tarnished or broken jewelry, business problems and disappointments. Loss of, warning of possible bad luck.

Journey ....Desire for pleasure, escape.

Judge ....If the judge is a familiar face, it may be someone you resent. If the case is against you, fear of failure. To win your case is a good omen.

Key ....Foretells a change. A broken key warns of sorrow. Lost key portends complications. To find a key is a lucky sign.

Kill ....The dreamer wishes to be rid of a difficult situation.

King ....Symbol of authority. To be one is a sign of desire to rule others. To talk to one means that you need guidance.

Kiss ....See "Embrace."

Kite ....Desire to socialize. A warning not to gamble.

Knife ....See "Dagger."

Knitting ....Indicates need for thrift. If by machine, a warning against hasty decisions.

Knots ....Minor worries.

Ladder ....See "Climbing," "Falling."
Lake ....Calm lake is a sign of romance, pleasure to come. Stormy lake indicates conflicts.
Lamb ....Symbol of happiness. Lost lamb, struggle for security.
Lamp ....Clear light is a sign of success.
Laughing ....Desire to escape worries.
Laundry ....Trifling problems.
Lawn ....See "Grass."
Lawyer ....See "Attorney," "Judge."
Letters ....A letter telling of bad news indicates that something is troubling the dreamer. He may be uncomfortable while dreaming, or he may be anticipating bad news.
Lightning ....A symbol of love.
Lion ....See "Animals."
Lobster ....Portends wealth.
Lock ....Dreamer wishes to look beyond lock.
Lost ....Frustration in love or money.
Lottery ....Desire for money. To win is a good omen.
Love ....Dreams of love usually mean that the dreamer is denied love during waking hours.
Machine gun .....See "Gun."
Machinery ....To fix machinery is a sign of good luck.
Mad dogs ....See "Dogs."
Magic ....See "Conjuror."
Mansion ....See "House."
Map ....Discontent with present surroundings.
Marriage ....A common dream for young people. For a married person to dream of another marriage or bigamy signifies distrust.
Mask ....Deception on the part of wearer.
Meals ....See "Eating."
Mice ....A warning of deception on part of friends.
Midget ....See "Dwarf."

Milk .... Symbol of abundance, good luck.
Minister .... See "Cardinal."
Mirror .... Warns of illness or loss to whomever you see.
Money .... Great desire for security.
Moon .... Symbol of love and harmony.
Mortgage .... To take a mortgage indicates lack of good economy. To hold one on someone else's property, a desire for great wealth.
Mortuary .... Unhappiness followed by rejoicing. Service for a stranger, anxiety over problem. For a member of family, it denotes good health despite worries.
Mother .... Symbol of protection, love. Dreams about mothers are common. To see your mother in various situations represents wishful thinking.
Mother-in-Law ... See "Mother."
Mountain .... See "Climbing."
Movies .... Desire for escape.
Murder .... To dream of this indicates that you do not want interference from the person, not that you really want to kill. To dream that you are murdered is a desire to be released from an uncomfortable situation.
Music .... To hear music you like portends good fortune.
Nakedness .... Desire to be noticed.
Navy .... Desire to escape present difficulties.
Necklace .... To find or receive one, a good omen.
Needle .... To thread one indicates responsibilities that require patience. To be sewing by hand indicates need of friends.
Nets .... To catch with, desire for binding contract. To get caught, desire to avoid entanglement. If torn, loss of some kind.

Newspaper ....To read one warns of danger to one's reputation.
Nuns ....For a woman, discontentment.
Nurse ....Omen of good health. To dream you are one indicates desire for friends.
Nuts ....To eat them is a prophecy that your wishes will be granted.
Oak ....Symbol of prosperity.
Oar ....To row, sacrifice, disappointment. To lose, useless effort.
Oatmeal ....A wish to rule others.
Oats ....A warning to finish what you start.
Ocean ....See "Lake," "Island."
Office ....To work in one, need for attention to business. To hold an office, high ambition.
Onions ....Opposition to present plans.
Opera ....See "Actor."
Oranges ....Omen of good health.
Orchard ....Symbol of love, happiness and achievement.
Orchestra ....To hear music of indicates much popularity for dreamer. To play in, a sign of advancement.
Organ ....To play, a sign of social honor and unusual awards. To hear music portends many friends.
Overcoat ....See "Coat."
Owl ....Gossip.
Oysters ....Tremendous desire for wealth.
Packing ....A repressed desire to travel and leave one's troubles behind.
Pagoda ....Desire to travel. See also, "House."
Painting ....To paint a picture of someone is to want to tell that person what you think of him.
Paralysis ....Inability to decide what to do.
Parents ....See "Father," "Mother."

Parrot .... See "Birds."
Party .... Desire to escape.
Passenger .... To be one, running away. To see others leaving without you, lost opportunity. To greet them, good luck.
Peaches .... Unattained wealth or love.
Pearls .... To find or receive, a good omen.
Pears .... Omen of good health.
Pebbles .... Petty jealousy, selfishness.
Pen, pencil .... Complications in love or money. Sex symbol.
Penny .... To dream of counting, warning to be careful with money.
Piano .... See "Music."
Pictures .... Desire for artistic expression.
Pilot .... Dreaming that you are one, a wish to direct others and be your own master.
Ping-Pong .... See "Baseball."
Pipe .... Omen of peaceful living. If broken, an omen of poor health or finances.
Pirate .... See "Bandit."
Pistol .... Sign of bad luck. See "Gun."
Pit .... Warning of hazards in job or marriage.
Pitcher .... Indicates physical thirst, desire to make new friends.
Plank .... Desire to reach goal that is out of reach at present.
Plow .... An uphill fight.
Plums .... See "Peaches," "Pears." Dried plum (prune) indicates dreamer should wait reasonable time before making decision.
Pocket(s) .... Signify desire to escape from reality.
Pocketbook .... Finding one signifies dreamer's wish for more money.
Poison .... Poison dreams indicate that the dreamer is looking for an easy way out.

Poker .... To stir up fire with indicates that the dreamer is industrious. See also "Gambling."

Police .... To see an officer, a desire to be protected. To be arrested, a guilt complex. To be arrested, though innocent, indicates over-anxiety.

Police dog .... See "Dogs."

Police station ..... See "Police," "Judge."

Pool .... See "Lake."

Pool (game) ...... See "Billiards."

Poppies .... See "Blossom."

Porter .... To see one indicates desire for travel, change.

Postman .... A sign of worries and possible complications.

Post office .... A reminder to do something you forgot.

Poultry .... See "Chickens."

Prayers .... Fear of failure.

Preacher .... See "Cardinal."

Pregnancy .... In women, wish fulfillment.

Priest .... See "Cardinal."

Prince, princess ... Aspirations, inferiority complex

Prison .... See "Jail."

Puppet .... See "Mask."

Purse .... See "Pocketbook."

Pursuit .... Dreams of being chased indicate a hidden fear. Dreams of running after something indicate an ambition of some sort.

Pyramids .... Desire for travel or new, possibly intellectual, interests.

Quarrels .... Portends complications in personal life.

Queen .... To dream that you are one signifies vanity. Otherwise, a queen is a symbol for a mother.

Rabbi .... See "Cardinal."

Railroad .... Winding tracks indicate problems in personal life.

Rain .... Storm indicates confusion. A summer shower is an omen of prosperity.

Rainbow .... A good omen.

Rape .... Unconscious wish fulfillment, for man or woman.

Rapids .... Worry that circumstances may be beyond your control. Desire to escape. Frustration.

Rat .... Deception. To kill, anger at false friend.

Razor .... See "Dagger."

Religion .... See "Church."

Reptiles .... See "Boa constrictor."

Restaurant .... Desire to be waited upon. Desire to socialize.

Revolver .... See "Gun."

Ribbons .... Desire for relaxation. For a girl, beware of flattery.

Rice .... Omen of wealth, happiness. Desire to mate.

Riding .... Bad omen. Desire for escape.

Ring .... Sign of friendship.

River .... See "Lake."

Road .... Adventures, pleasant or unpleasant, depending on the terrain.

Rocking chair ..... To sit in one, a sign of contentment. To see an empty one indicates sorrow.

Roof .... To be building or reaching for one indicates great ambition. To be on top of one indicates unusually good opportunities are presenting themselves to you.

Room .... A hidden fear. Possibly, symbol of a woman.

Rooster .... To see one, a good omen. To hear one, a sign of conceit.

Rope ....Sign of risky venture. To tie rope, a wish to rule others.

Roses ....See "Blossom."

Running ....See "Pursuit."

Saddle ....Good omen. Also desire for change, escape.

Sailing ....See "Lake."

Sailors ....Desire for change, escape.

Saw ....Sign of good sense and resourcefulness.

Scaffold ....Warning about possible imprudent actions.

Scales ....Good judgment. Sign of faithfulness in love.

School ....You feel you are being tested and you are worried.

Schoolteacher ....Symbol of authority. Possible interest in matters intellectual. To be one, a desire to rule others.

Scissors ....Sign of jealousy, distrust in marriage. See also, "Dagger."

Scrapbook ....Desire to escape into the past.

Scratch ....To scratch is to criticize. To be scratched indicates petty annoyances.

Sculptor ....Artistic turn of mind.

Sea ....See "Lake."

Seal ....On a letter, means your mind is made up. To see a seal (animal) indicates uncertainty.

Searching ....Sign of loss, or fear of loss.

Serpent ....See "Alligator."

Servant ....To dream that you employ one is a good omen.

Shampoo ....Warning not to repeat gossip. See "Bath."

Shark ....Possible financial difficulties. See "Animals."

Shawl ....See "Cape," "Coat."

Shears ....See "Scissors."

Sheep ....Sign of prosperity ahead.
Shells ....To gather, a sign of thrift.
Shelter ....Desire to escape enemies. Unconscious guilt.
Shelves ....If filled, good omen. If empty, possible loss or disappointment.
Sheriff ....See "Police."
Ship ....Desire for escape. A tossing ship may have hidden sexual implications.
Shirt ....See "Coat."
Shoes ....See "Coat."
Shooting ....See "Gun."
Shot ....Possible misfortune ahead.
Shotgun ....See "Gun."
Shovel ....You are a good worker.
Shower ....See "Rain."
Silk ....Sign of love and friendship. Good omen.
Silverware ....Discontent.
Skates ....Desire for escape.
Skeleton ....Secrets that you are suppressing.
Skull ....See "Skeleton."
Sky ....Condition of sky indicates your mood.
Sled ....See "Skates."
Sliding ....You're letting matters get out of your control.
Slippers ....See "Coat."
Smoke ....Indicates confusion; seek guidance.
Snakes ....Sex urge.
Snow ....Portends disappointments.
Soap ....Desire for fresh start.
Sold ....Business worries.
Soldiers ....Desire for advancement. If wounded, possible losses due to bad judgment.
Son ....If dutiful, high aspirations. If ill or absent, anguish.

Soup ....Good omen.
Spade ....See "Shovel."
Spectacles ....Symbol of authority, good judgment.
Spider ....A worrisome obstacle. See "Ants."
Spools ....Worrisome obstacles.
Spoons ....Good omen. To lose, possible misfortune.
Sports ....See "Baseball."
Spy ....Sign of anxiety.
Squirrels ....You are overly concerned with security. You are looking forward to a busy time.
Stage ....See "Movies."
Stains ....Worry over small difficulties.
Stairs ....Walking up, good fortune. Down, many obstacles.
Stars ....Good omen, except shooting stars which augur trouble.
Stealing ....Desire to possess something unattainable.
Steps ....See "Stairs."
Stones ....Obstacles. If thrown, a sign of fear.
Store ....Desire for pleasure.
Storm ....See "Rain."
Stove ....Desire for love and protection.
Stranger ....Fear of misfortune.
Street ....To walk down, desire to advance. To stand on, perplexity.
Sugar ....Desire to forget troubles.
Suicide ....Desire to escape troubles.
Sun ....A good omen, if rising or shining. Through clouds, good times ahead.
Swamp ....Sign of unhappiness, uncertainty.
Swan ....Good omen.
Sweeping ....Desire to please others.
Swimming ....If enjoyed, a good omen. If difficult, you feel you are faced with overwhelming difficulties.

Sword ....See "Dagger."
Table ....If full of food, a good omen. If full of papers, much work or many bills.
Tea ....Beware of gossip.
Teacher ....If you see one, you may be seeking advice. See "Schoolteacher."
Tears ....See "Crying."
Teeth ....Good teeth, good omen.
Telegram ....Portends disagreeable news.
Telephone ....If you hear it ring, someone long absent may soon contact you. To talk on phone indicates desire to improve circumstances.
Telescope ....You are looking for new opportunities.
Television ....See "Movies."
Tennis ....To play is a yearning for popularity. To win is a good omen. To lose, a bad omen.
Tent ....Desire for change of environment.
Terror ....Indicates fear of some person or situation in real life.
Theater ....See "Movies."
Thief ....To see one indicates that you feel that someone is deceiving you. To be one indicates financial difficulties.
Thimble ....Minor worries.
Thread ....May indicate losses due to overkindness.
Tiger ....See "Animals."
Tobacco ....If smoking or watching someone smoke, a sign of peace, harmony and contentment.
Torture ....Struggles and disappointment in love or money.
Toy ....A good omen, except if broken.
Train ....Desire for escape.
Tramp ....Fear of failure.
Travel . ...Desire for pleasure, escape.
Trees ....A good omen, except if in bad condition.

Trunk .... Desire for change. If locked, thwarted ambitions.

Tunnel .... To see, feeling of insecurity. To be trapped in, desire to escape or a feeling of being trapped. Also a symbol of sexual interest.

Turkey .... Sign of abundance.

Ulcer .... A simple sign of worry.

Umbrella .... Symbol of difficulties. If it is raining, an open umbrella represents a friend.

University .... See "College."

Valentine .... Desire for love, thoughts of marriage.

Vase .... If filled with flowers, a good omen. If broken, sorrow.

Vegetables .... If fresh, a good omen.

Veil .... If you are wearing, a guilt complex. Otherwise it represents unsolved problems.

Ventriloquist ..... You do not believe what you have heard.

Vineyard .... A good omen.

Violin .... To play denotes desire for recognition. See "Music."

Volcano .... Sign that you need to control your emotions.

Waiter .... See "Restaurant."

Wake .... Feeling of helplessness, frustration.

Walking .... To dream that you are walking on a rough or winding path forebodes distress.

Wall .... Sign of frustration, inability to attain ambition. Breaking through, a good omen.

Wallet .... Desire for pleasures requiring money.

Waltzing .... See "Dancing."

War .... Sign of family disputes.

Wasp .... See "Ants."

Watch .... Altogether a good omen.

Water .... To dream that you are drinking may indicate that you are actually thirsty, though asleep. Clear water, good omen. Muddy water, misfortune. To play in, desire for relaxation. To jump in, a hope for another opportunity.

Web ....See "Spider."
Wedding ....See "Marriage."
Window ....If closed, frustration. If broken, disappointment. To crawl through, dishonorable intentions.
Wolf ....Suspicion of hidden enemies.
Woods ....A good omen, unless on fire, in which case a warning to prepare for your welfare.
Workshop ....To dream about one indicates a desire to take matters in hand and help yourself surmount difficulties.
Worms ....See "Snakes."
Wreath ....A good omen.
X ray ....Overconcern with health, or desire to know motives of associates.
Yacht ....Desire to escape reality.
Zoo ....Indicates a feeling of helplessness.

OMENS!

In the past few pages, we have seen some of the ways the Master Mind reveals His signs to you. While it is not possible to predict the exact sign He will send you, many of His signs do have certain specific characteristics. I have tried to indicate these in the past few chapters, beginning with the techniques of spirit contact.

Among these signs are *omens.* Omens are happenings that are thought to foreshadow important events. There are natural omens, like flood or drought, and artificial omens, like the throw of dice. Both may have meaning. First an omen occurs, followed by the event it foreshadowed.

Whether an omen foretells good or evil, it is truly a Godsend in that such a sign makes it possible to *prepare* for—and therefore *soften* the blow—if the hardship is unavoidable, or even steer completely clear of it.

Too few people heed these signs of the Master Mind. If they did, think how much hardship and suffering could be avoided. Had we been adequately prepared for the Second World War, for example, the enemy might have been vanquished in but a fraction of the time it actually took to build up our supplies. The war lasted four years, more than half of which was spent just trying to fend the enemy off while we built the needed ships, planes and ammunition.

And yet the Master Mind sent us many signs beforehand, among them . . .

THE ARMORED HORSEMAN OF CHISHOLM HOLLOW

Soon after the central Texas hill country was settled, Indians and white men began hearing mysterious sounds, like metal striking metal, from a small valley or hollow in the area. Most folks wrote the reports off as fairy tales, but none dared to go near the place. One settler, however, finally did go into the valley to track down some wolves. After dismounting from his horse to examine the animal tracks, he was startled by the clank of metal and the sound of horse's hooves. There, galloping through the valley, was a knight in shining armor, brandishing a lance, and riding a white steed! But this was almost the 20th Century!

The Armored Horseman of Chisholm Hollow is a strange apparition that the people of the central Texas hills have seen before every major conflict in which the United States has become involved, from the Civil War right on down to the present. He thunders out of the valley, makes an appearance, then vanishes, all in plain sight.

OTHER EXAMPLES

Perhaps the strangest omens of all time were those connected with President Kennedy's death. For one thing, amazing similarities existed between President Kennedy's administration and that of President Lincoln.

- Both were concerned with Civil Rights.
- Lincoln was elected in 1860, Kennedy in 1960.
- Both were slain on a Friday in the presence of their wives.
- Their successors were both named Johnson.
- Andrew Johnson was born in 1808; Lyndon Johnson was born in 1908.
- Lincoln's secretary, whose name was Kennedy, advised him not to go to the theater the night he was killed (indeed, Lincoln himself had had a dream about a presidential assassination a week before). President Kennedy's secretary, whose name was Lincoln, advised him not to go to Dallas, as did many other administration officials.
- A very strange omen is the fact that the President and Mrs. Kennedy were forced to sleep in separate rooms the night before the assassination.
- Hundreds of people, including myself, had premonitions concerning President Kennedy's safety, although we didn't know why. Washington's famed seeress, Jeane Dixon, publicly predicted the likelihood of an assassination four years before it happened, and again a month before it happened. Billy Graham, the well-known evangelist, is quoted as saying, "I had the strongest premonition that he should not go to Texas," and he tried desperately to warn the President.
- The President himself must have had premonitions of it. The Hearst Headline Service reported only a few

months before a remark attributed to the President: "I wonder if they'll shoot me in church." And in March, 1963, while on a visit to Arlington National Cemetery, President Kennedy said: "The view up here is so beautiful, I could stay here forever."

As if all this weren't enough, all astrological forecasts for the President were dark at the time.

THE MAN WHO IGNORED OMENS

For those of you who are inclined to pooh-pooh these manifestations of spiritual guidance, and say that they are only for the superstitious, there is the story of Marcello N., reported in the papers recently. Marcello, too, decided that this was a primitive attitude, and resolved to ignore the signs of the Master Mind. While walking down a Rome, Italy, street, he noticed a ladder which was being used by a workman to make alterations on a building. Marcello deliberately decided to walk under the ladder, and started to cross the street toward it.

Just at that point, Marcello later recalled, traffic became very heavy and he had to wait (an omen). A patrolman waved him forward and Marcello, about to cross the street, felt a stitch of pain in his side (another omen). "Must be something I ate," he thought, pausing briefly, and he continued, heading straight for the ladder. Just then a stranger hailed him and remarked, "Better watch it. Those things are dangerous." (A *third* warning!)

Marcello waved him off and stepped directly under the ladder. Just then a workman above lost his grip on a hammer and the heavy tool promptly fell on Marcello's head.

• • •

The Master Mind punishes no one. He tries to help us every way He can. It is we who in ignoring these Cosmic Signs and deliberately flouting His help punish ourselves

As a fitting ending to these pages, I would like you to read and dwell upon the meaning of some words, written by a young man from beyond, who came back, in a famous recorded case. It says to me that *love* is the difference between *life* and a living death. And that the more love a person has, the higher his evolution and development is. And the higher his development is, the closer he is to knowledge of God, and the meaning of life.

> The noblest work on earth, within my ken
> Is ministering to the souls of men.
> And if our vision's true and God is near,
> His voice will speak to you and you will hear,
> "Go ye out to all the world and preach for me
> The Gospel of Immortality."
> For God's in every man and man's divine
> For He hath said, "Let thy light so shine,"
> That unto all others a beacon it shall be,
> Helping and guiding on toward Immortality.
> Thou canst not help or guide the least one on
> If thou are not sure thyself the way is true;
> That is the reason I have come to you
> To make it simpler, clearer, unto thee,
> To find the way to Immortality.
> If thou hast helped just one poor, lonely soul
> To heal a wound and make it whole,
> Then hast thou seen God, and God shall dwell
> with thee,
> Making thee sure of Immortality.*

These words have haunted me, and have actually set the goal of my life. I hope they do the same for you. If you have learned to love and appreciate the natural forces and powers with which we are blessed—through anything in these pages—go out and preach the Gospel of Immortality in your own way.

---

* S. Ralph Harlow and Evan Hill, *A Life After Death* (New York City, N.Y.: Doubleday & Co., 1961), reprinted by permission.

SUMMARY OF TELECULT POWER #10

1. Your helpers in the invisible world try to arrange circumstances in your favor—even if you deny their existence and spurn their help.
2. One of the ways in which you are helped in your everyday life is in the form of signs or suggestions.
3. Spirit signs always point the way to opportunities, which if acted upon, literally push you ahead to success with little or no effort.
4. All day long, you are being literally bombarded with wonderful, magical, transforming signs—invisible to you now, but clear as life and plain as day when you take one simple step—which, if heeded, would make your life a heaven on earth.
5. The first giant step in recognizing these Cosmic Signs is simply to admit the possibility that they come.
6. The next step is to realize that no matter what form the sign takes, it will invariably be the one most appropriate to the occasion, and most easily recognizable to you.
7. The last step is the easiest of all. Do exactly what the sign tells you to do—remembering that this sign is like "power steering": it will literally push you ahead to success with little or no effort.
8. There is only one way to "deal with the devil" in life, and that is to *believe*—if not in the Master Mind, at least in the possibility of ultimate good.
9. Try to look on the bright side of things. Try to see the good in every situation. As soon as you do this, a world of wonder and beauty and golden opportunities opens to you. And it becomes a very simple matter, indeed, to see the Master Mind's signs.
10. While it is not possible to predict the exact signs that will be revealed to you, most of them fall into six main cate-

gories: the Signs of Love, the Signs of Prosperity, the Signs of Right, the Signs of Wrong, the Signs of Danger, the Signs of Salvation. Examples of each are given in this chapter.

11. Another method you can use to receive Cosmic Signs is to make a Tele-Photo Transmitter—as revealed in this chapter—to see people and events in your future. This is possible because, to the extent that Cosmic Intelligence tries to arrange circumstances in your favor, your future *is* predetermined. This means that certain people, places and events are actually moving toward you. Opportunities for love, prosperity, and happiness will be presented to you. You have but to recognize them.
12. This chapter reveals a "Magic Ring" that lets you talk with animals.
13. In these pages, you'll also discover the meaning of 500 Dreams! Dreams are signs of a special sort—they are our link with the nether world of the spirit. In dreams, you can take fantastic astral journeys into the past, present, or future.
14. The reason that many dreams have specific meanings that can be listed here is that part of every dream is your reaction to it. Psychologists have discovered that similar dreams tend to occur in the minds of many people, and that the second part—what people make of the messages in their dreams—tends to have the same or similar meaning.
15. Among the signs you can receive are Omens. Omens are happenings that are thought to foreshadow important events. There are natural omens, like flood or drought, and artificial omens, like the throw of dice. Both may have meaning. First an omen occurs, followed by the event it foreshadowed.
16. Whether an omen foretells good or evil, it is truly a God-send in that such a sign makes it possible to *prepare* for—and therefore *soften* the blow—if the hardship is unavoidable, or even steer completely clear of it.

9 788125 500254

Printed at Repro India Ltd.